CW01370251

# Wines of Malta
## The Essential Guide

# Wines of Malta
## The Essential Guide

*to Jim Budd*

*Best Wishes!*

*[signature] Dec-06*

### Georges Meekers
Foreword by Serge Dubs

Wines of Malta - The Essential Guide

Text Copyright © – Georges Meekers

Photos & Design Copyright © - Miller Distributors Limited

First edition 2006

ISBN-10: 99932-86-11-7
ISBN-13: 978-99932-86-11-0

Published by Miller Distributors Limited
'Miller House', Tarxien Road, Airport Way, Luqa, Malta.
Tel: (+356) 21 664 488  Fax: (+356) 21 676 799
e-mail: info@millermalta.com  web: www.millermalta.com

Photography by Kevin Casha FMIPP FSWPP AMPS AMPA LBIPP

Design & Layout by Daniel Borg

Printing by Gutenberg Press Limited

*All rights reserved. No part of this book may be reproduced or transmitted in any form or any means, electronic or mechanical, including photocopying, recording, or by any form of p2p transmission, storage and retrieval system, without permission in writing from the author.*

# Contents

|  | FOREWORD BY SERGE DUBS | Pg 6 |
|---|---|---|
| 1. | **UPFRONT** | |
|  | EARLY BEGINNINGS | Pg 12 |
| 2. | **DEFINING MALTA** | |
|  | GETTING ACQUAINTED | Pg 16 |
|  | WATER, ANYONE? | Pg 20 |
|  | GIVE ME LAND… | Pg 24 |
| 3. | **LOOKING BACK** | |
|  | MERRY FIELD BLENDS | Pg 29 |
|  | ON THE WINGS OF PHYLLOXERA | Pg 31 |
|  | ONE MAN'S MEAT… | Pg 34 |
|  | HOW IT WAS | Pg 37 |
| 4. | **STEPPING STONES** | |
|  | BY MEANS OF SCARCITY | Pg 42 |
|  | SHAPING A TASTE FOR VARIETY | Pg 45 |
| 5. | **VITICULTURAL REVIVAL** | |
|  | GOODNESS GRAPES ME! | Pg 50 |
|  | VINES FOR WINES | Pg 55 |
|  | CHAMPIONING WINES | Pg 58 |
| 6. | **FOSTERING QUALITY** | |
|  | YOU, THE CONSUMER | Pg 62 |
| 7. | **GRAPE AWAKENINGS** | |
|  | MALTA'S VERY OWN GRAPES: | Pg 72 |
|  | THE G-FORCE ĠELLEWŻA AND GIRGENTINA | Pg 75 |
|  | THE NEW GRAPES ON THE BLOCK: | Pg 79 |
|  | THE INTERNATIONAL VARIETIES | Pg 81 |
| 8. | **IN A GLASS OF THEIR OWN** | |
|  | CLEAR CUT | Pg 106 |
|  | BASIC TASTING CUES | Pg 116 |
| 9. | **NIPPED IN THE BUD** | |
|  | BETWEEN MADEIRA AND LA MANCHA | Pg 120 |
|  | HOW TO FIND OUT MORE | Pg 126 |
|  | BIBLIOGRAPHY AND FURTHER READING | Pg 127 |
|  | INDEX | Pg 129 |

# Préface

C'est avec plaisir que j'apporte mon soutien à Georges, auteur du livre au sujet des vins de Malte que vous tenez entre les mains. Excellente idée que celle d'un guide des vins qui lui permet de partager avec les amateurs du monde entier sa connaissance de l'industrie vinicole et des vins maltais, encore très peu répandus à l'étranger.

J'ai personnellement découvert les vins maltais il y a une quinzaine d'années à Vinexpo à Bordeaux. Ce fut pour moi une formidable découverte mais surtout un véritable plaisir gustatif.
La dégustation de ces vins maltais bien produits a partir de raisins gorgés de soleil m'a permis de mieux comprendre le passé viticole et les nouvelles techniques des producteurs maltais. Ces derniers sont aujourd'hui capables de rivaliser avec les régions viticoles beaucoup mieux connues.

En fait, lorsqu'on goute aux vins maltais, on n'a qu'une seule envie: boucler ses valises et aller visiter ce minuscule archipel situé au cœur de la Méditerranée et qui peut se vanter d'avoir un immense héritage culturel ainsi que des traditions millénaires.

Ma première dégustation de vins maltais m'a amenée à essayer des vins issus de cépages dits internationaux: Chardonnay, Cabernet Sauvignon, Syrah et Merlot. Ensuite, lors de ma visite du vignoble maltais, j'ai également eu l'occasion d'apprécier les vins maltais produits à base de cépages autochtones: Girgentina et Ġellewża.

J'ai été agréablement surpris de constater que ces vins aussi avaient leurs propres personnalité, originalité et arômes uniques qui plairont tant aux néophytes qu'aux professionnels.

Ils font intégralement partie de l'immense diversité et de l'éventail culturel du monde du vin. J'insiste par ailleurs sur le fait que les vins produits a partir de cépages spécifiques a certaines régions exprimant leur propre caractère doivent continuer à exister. Les vins maltais issus de cépages maltais ne devraient pas tomber dans l'oubli.

Faire connaître les vins de Malte (aussi bien ceux provenant de cépages internationaux qu'autochtones) au grand public n'est sans doute pas pour demain.

Mais pour la première fois, il existe un livre qui décrit leur goût inimitable et les replace dans l'histoire du vin. Georges a écrit ce guide des vins de Malte avec passion et sérieux. Il vous sera très utile dans la découverte des vins que proposent ces magnifiques îles maltaises que je vous encourage vivement à visiter.

Je vous souhaite un merveilleux voyage et puissiez-vous trouver sur votre route de belles découvertes et beaucoup de nouveaux vins à déguster.

Santé!

Serge Dubs
*Sommelier*
*Meilleur Sommelier du Monde 1989*

# Foreword

It is with pleasure that I support Georges' book about the wines of Malta that you are holding now. His publication is an excellent idea, an essential guide book, and also a practical tool to let wine lovers around the world share in his knowledge of Malta's wine industry and wines which are not yet widely available overseas.

Personally, I discovered and tasted Malta's wines for the first time some fifteen years ago at Vinexpo in Bordeaux. It was a great unearthing apart from a real gustatory pleasure. Tasting these well-made Malta grown wines from sun-kissed grapes has enhanced my understanding of the Island's vineyard husbandry and the newly gained skills of Maltese winemakers. They are now capable of producing wines on par with many other wines from more famous wine producing countries.

In fact, sampling Malta's wines makes one wish to pack his bags and visit this tiny archipelago situated in the heart of the Mediterranean Sea that can boast of an immense cultural heritage and age-old traditions, too.

The first Malta grown wines I assessed were made from so-called international grape varieties: Chardonnay, Cabernet Sauvignon, Syrah and Merlot. But later, when I actually visited the Maltese Islands and the land under vine, I also took the opportunity to sample those Maltese wines made from the country's indigenous grape varieties, namely Girgentina and Ġellewża. And, I was pleasantly surprised since these wines, too, show off their own personality, originality and unique flavours. They very well may enchant many wine enthusiasts and wine experts alike.

They are part and parcel of the rich diversity and cultural palette of the wine world. I therefore support the idea that wines made from particular grape varieties that are the prerogative of a certain region which express their clean characteristics keep on existing. Maltese wines made from grape varieties native to Malta only should not have to fade away.

Making Malta's wines - made from either international or indigenous grape varieties - commonly known to the wine drinker at large will of course not happen overnight.

But here is for the first time a book that explains their inimitable taste and their place in the history of wine. Georges has written this essential guide to the wines of Malta with passion and dedication. It will be instrumental in the discovery of the vinous offering of the beautiful Maltese Islands which I encourage you to visit.

I wish you a fabulous journey and many discoveries along your path. May you find countless wines to taste.

Cheers!

Serge Dubs
*Sommelier*
*World's Best Sommelier 1989*

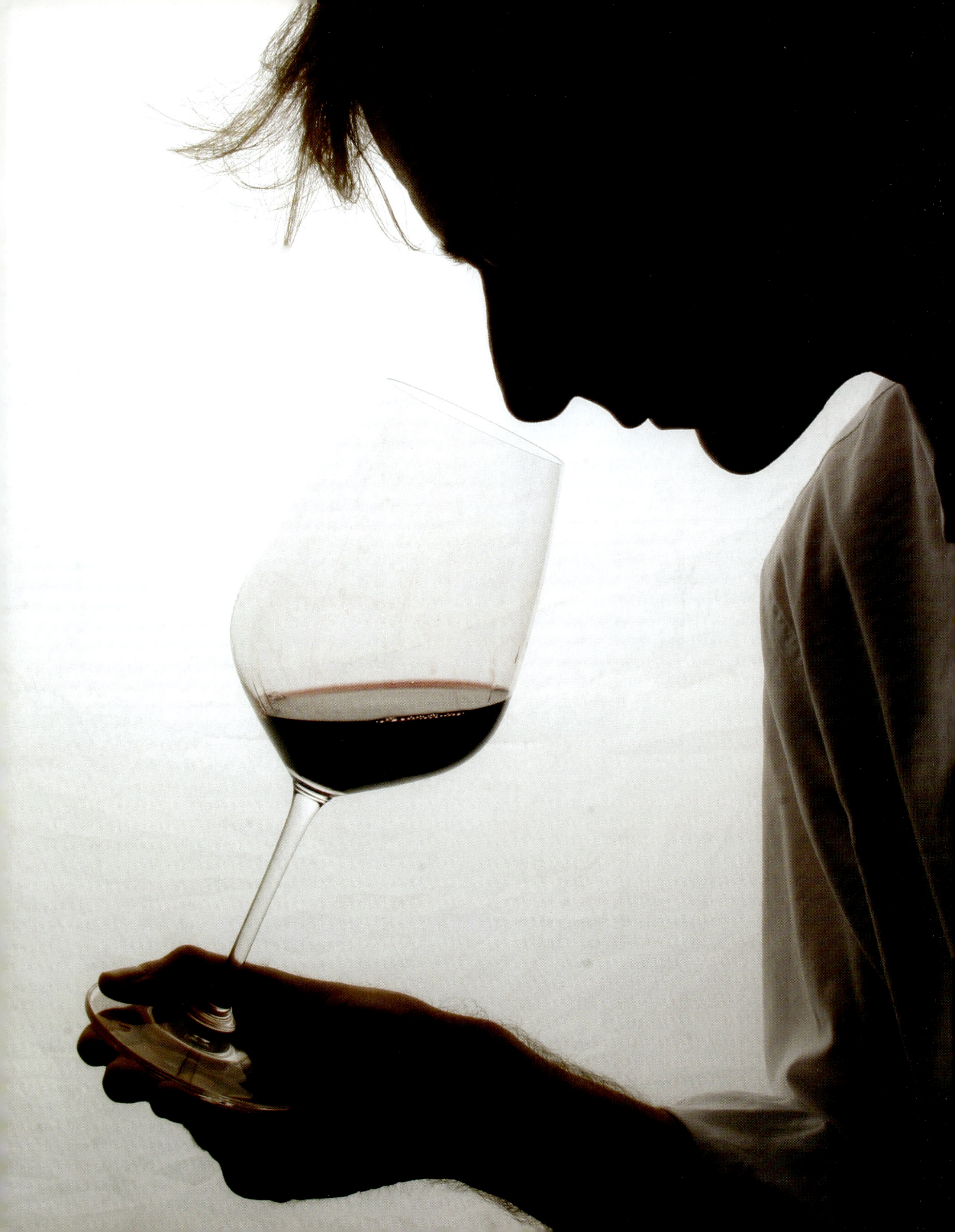

# Acknowledgements

**DEDICATED TO MY CHILDREN IKE AND LEAH "MAY THEY NEVER LACK CHARACTER; THEIR SPIRIT NEVER BREAK, THEIR CONFIDENCE GROW STRONGER"**

Many people have, often accidentally, contributed to this book, which ironically owes its existence in part to the irritating tenacity of few wine snobs and pseudo critics that boorishly eyebrow Maltese wines.

I cannot thank them nor can I express my gratitude to everyone by name that has assisted in the writing of this book more intentionally by generously giving time, information and guidance. However, I thank them all the same.

Without the continuous support of my ever more astounding wife Stefie my untiring passion for wine would never have transpired in this publication.

Sincere thanks also to the publishing team at Miller Distributors for consideration of my manuscript and for carrying it through to its acceptance for publication.

I also wish to acknowledge the wonderful creative work photographer Kevin Casha and designer Daniel Borg have delivered to 'put the book together and bring my writings visually alive'.

Finally, I extend my earnest thanks to many others in the vineyards and cellars, and all those along the production lines of the wines I have had the pleasure of tasting and evaluating.

Georges Meekers

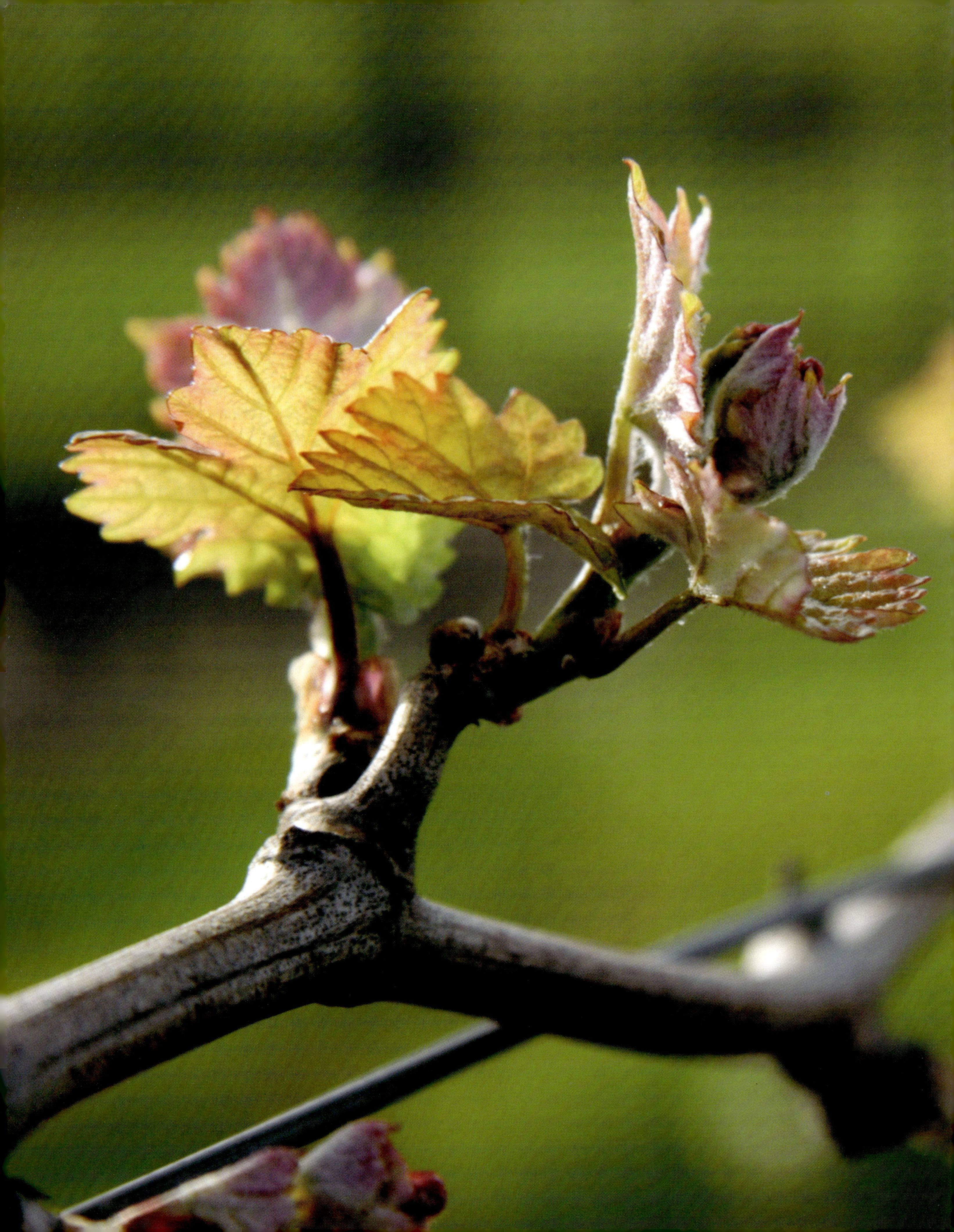

# Upfront

The Maltese have grown vines and produced wine for well over 4000 years, since the arrival of foreign invaders such as the seafaring Phoenicians, the Romans, the Arabs and the Knights of the Order of St. John of Jerusalem. The legacy continues.

# Early Beginnings

"To take wine into our mouths is to savour a droplet of the river of human history". These wise words by wine-loving radio and television entertainer Clifton Paul Fadiman certainly apply to the wines of Malta and the country's action-packed past.

The tiny Maltese archipelago of three inhabited islands named Malta, Gozo and Comino lies at the crossroads of the Mediterranean Sea between Sicily and North Africa. With an area totalling barely 316 square kilometres, the Maltese Islands may be small in size but they have been the playing field of foreign invaders for many centuries.

Due to its strategic position, Malta's history has presented a constant struggle for the population that now stands at around 398,000 inhabitants. In fact, Malta's history has always been a challenging one and so has the art of grape growing and winemaking in the Maltese Islands.

Malta's connection with wine began when prehistoric peoples learned to store some of the abundant summer fruits to tide them over the bleak winter months. Some of these fruits would have been wild grapes, perhaps stored in a hollow rock. The sugary juice would have come in contact with the natural yeasts sitting on the skins of the grapes and, as if by magic, transformed into an alcoholic beverage: wine.

While the exact beginnings will probably never be known, the Maltese Islands' viticulture (the art of grape growing) has millenarian origins.

The Phoenicians, thought to have been one of the earliest wine-producing civilisations, probably arrived in the Eastern Mediterranean about 3000 B.C. For thousands of years, these fearless and seafaring people spread their influence throughout the Mediterranean, Europe and even beyond into the Atlantic.

Grape vines came to be introduced in the colonies in many coastal areas where the Phoenicians settled. As the Phoenicians were one of the earliest people known to have populated the Maltese Islands, from 800–480 B.C., the Maltese archipelago can boast of being one of the earliest places in the Mediterranean to actually cultivate grapes.

By classical times, vines were grown for winemaking in almost all the Mediterranean countries. From Spain in the West to Byblos in the East, from northern Italy to North Africa, the cultivated grape made inexorable progress, with amphorae regularly crossing the sea. Historically, the Mediterranean was indeed the hub of viticulture and most of the wines in those days came from the countries in the Mediterranean basin that were blessed with ideal climatic conditions.

By 218 B.C. Malta had become part of the Roman Empire. The Romans propagated the cult of their god of wine, Bacchus, to

all corners of their empire, developing a flourishing wine trade even beyond the Mediterranean shores. So sophisticated was their knowledge of viticulture and oenology (the knowledge of wine and winemaking) that their techniques were not equalled until the 17th or 18th centuries when the Italians, French and other Europeans began to regard the making of wine as science, rather than a mystery.
As the Roman Empire crumbled, winemaking slipped away into Maltese memory, along with much of the civilization the Romans had introduced.

People began to fight for survival. Indications show that there was a near-complete break with ancestral tradition, even in agriculture. Deforestation and soil erosion soon set in.

By the time the North African Berbers, spearheading the expansion of Islam, had taken over the Maltese Islands in around A.D. 870, the land had become barren. The Arabs brought with them citrus fruits and cotton, as well as the basis of the modern Maltese language.

Although they introduced innovative agricultural systems such as irrigation, it was difficult for the 'dielja' (Maltese for 'vine') to survive under the reign of the new rulers whose religious Muslim beliefs did not favour winemaking.

The dark Middle Ages were characterized by the invasions and pirate attacks that depopulated the islands. The spread of malaria, fever epidemics and the plague, as well as the emigration to Sicily and Italy eventually led once more to the abandonment of cultivated land. Every time Malta experienced a difficult period, winemaking suffered another setback.

In 1524, the Knights of the Order of St. John of Jerusalem sent their scouts to give Malta the once-over as a possible settlement. They had been thrown out of Rhodes and were looking for another place to make their base. But the isles had become no more than sandstone rocks, the surface of which was barely covered with five feet of earth. Although not very keen, the Knights had no choice but to come to Malta, and they were given the Islands from the Emperor of Spain in exchange for a rent of two Maltese falcons a year.

As they set about creating those aspects of civilization to which they had become accustomed, they tried to rehabilitate the abandoned agricultural areas. Wine, apart from being a necessary adjunct to Holy Mass, was also one of their daily staples and on their list of importation requirements.

It was during this time that the wine trade and winemaking in Malta made a comeback, once the Knights had established wine as a popular drink. The Order created land-leasing schemes for farmers in order to increase the number of cultivated fields to feed the expanding local population. More fields were created by means of terracing.

Another downturn for wine was on the horizon. The increased demand for cotton in the nineteenth century, when Malta was under British rule, and especially during the time of the American War of Secession, led to the grubbing-up of the Maltese vineyards and olive groves to make room for its cultivation.

Only towards the 1870s was the farming of vines resumed. Twenty years later there were considerable vineyards at Xaghra, Nadur, Qala, Żebbuġ and elsewhere in Gozo, as well as in the districts of Mdina, Dingli, Fiddien, Ġnejna, Bahrija and Mellieha in Malta.

Somehow, the vine has managed to survive in Malta through the Great Siege of the Ottoman Turks, followed by the arrival of Napoleon and the onslaught of World War II, when the Maltese met fearsome bombardment with bravery and perseverance, throughout the British regime and the turbulent early days of Maltese autonomy and independence. After all, winemaking is a legacy in Malta, it is in the blood, and, as always, it will go on.

# Defining Malta

Malta, the tiny rock in the centre of the Mediterranean Sea, might not be the first country that springs to the mind of the continental wine drinker.
Yet, Malta is very much at the heart of Mediterranean wine growing.

# Getting Acquainted

Malta's vineyards are suitably situated on the 35th parallel in the northern hemisphere and have their roots in small terraced fields. Malta is located in the middle of the Mediterranean Sea at 93 kilometres from Sicily and 290 kilometres from Tunisia. The Maltese land is a natural habitat for the vine.

Generally speaking, for grapes to grow happily, commercial vineyard areas need to be located in two broad bands in the northern and southern hemispheres, roughly between 30° and 50° latitude. It is here that a balance between warmth, sunshine and rainfall is found to create the ideal growing conditions for the vine and the ripening of its fruit.

Malta fits the ticket perfectly. It is a pity, really, that there isn't more land under vine available to produce sufficient quantities of grapes for wine to supply the volume-demanding wine merchants on the European mainland.
The modern wines are, without exaggeration, excellent.

The total landmass of this tiny group of islands is merely comparable to the Isle of Wight, UK or Martha's Vineyard, USA, with the longest distance in Malta being about 27 kilometres. The vineyards are as a result, tiny and range in size from a tenth of a hectare to around 20 hectares. Malta only gained independence from Britain in 1964 – one year after Italian lawmakers passed the law that introduced the concept of Denominazione di Origine Controllata (DOC) in Italy. Meanwhile Malta has become a member of the European Union, where the choice of grape varieties available to vignerons and vintners of its member states is narrowed down to only those permitted by law.

For example, in Burgundy, France, a winemaker must source the Pinot Noir or the Gamay for his red wines, and the Chardonnay or the Aligoté for his whites. If he wants to make red Hermitage in the Rhône, he is forced to use the Syrah, and any producer that wants to make Vouvray in the Loire, needs to draw on the Chenin Blanc. Pretty much the same system is in place in Italy and other member states.

In the new EU member-state Malta, where modern viticulture has only just begun to bud, the choice of grape varieties has very much been left up to the vintners and growers and is for the time being at least still based on the prevailing market demands and conditions dominant in the vineyard.

Although the Maltese government, together with the growers and winemakers, has formalized the list of permissible grape varieties, choosing what grape variety actually to plant remains as always a science in itself and has to be done thoughtfully.
The choice of which grape variety to plant will depend on the soil, site and exposure to the elements, as well as the overall climate and the vineyard's micro-climate.

DEFINING MALTA

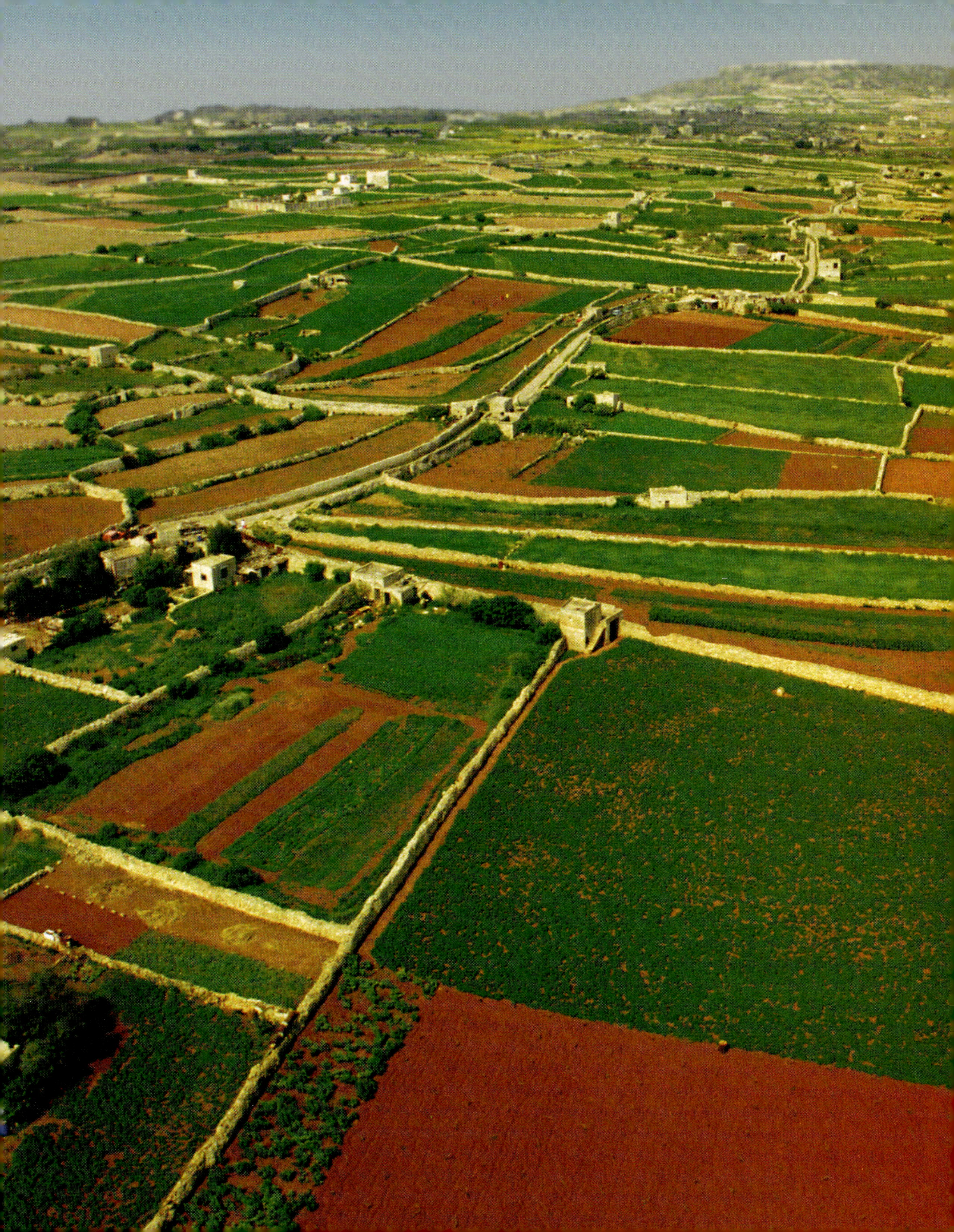

In the world of wine, there are many different theories about how to plant a vineyard. In Malta, where a series of low hills with small, terraced fields on slopes characterize the terrain, one needs to take into account all the problems inherent with the Maltese agricultural situation, such as land fragmentation and owner diversity. Some agricultural plots can be as tiny as a tenth of a hectare and a large number of plots are not owned but leased by full- and part-time farmers.

Grape growers or vignerons, for example, seldom have the luxury of making the rows of vines follow the contours of the small fields so as to minimize soil erosion. Traditional rubble walls take care of that.
Enough exposure to the sun isn't a preoccupation of the growers in sun-drenched Malta, but shelter for the vines from the prevailing northwesterly winds is.

The wind strength is not usually strong, except during winter storms when the vine is dormant anyway. They are felt in gusts and can do little damage to the vine shoots during late April and May. Certainly, the low bush method of vine training used for the two unique native varieties Girgentina (white) and Ġellewża (black) must have evolved and been favoured in part for this reason.

Nowadays, other international grape varieties are being cultivated as well. Cabernet, Merlot and Chardonnay, for example, need the system of elevated training along wires with drip irrigation. The Maltese landscape is slowly changing. Patches of fields dotted with the indigenous bush trained varieties are being surrounded by larger vineyards where international grape varieties native to a number of different regions, soils and climates in France and Italy, grow almost side-by-side on trellises.

It is a delightful sight, especially when looking down on the island of Malta from the air. On the approach, one sees the steep western cliffs rise to heights of about 253 metres, whereas the narrow valleys on the southeast coast are submerged and form deep harbours. Malta is a low, tilted plateau of limestone strata. The northern part of the island is crossed by a series of parallel faults, which have produced a number of small rift valleys that are favoured for agricultural use.

In the sister island; Gozo, the costal uplift is not so pronounced and the wide slopes spread out of the hard coralline rock Its smaller size and lack of harbours has restricted Gozo's development to being a wholly agricultural economy. Comino is the smallest of the three inhabited islands with nearly 2.8 square kilometres land surface and even here the vine has taken root.

The Maltese climate is obviously very Mediterranean. Over one million sun-seeking visitors travel to Malta each year to enjoy the sun. Summers are long, hot and dry. There is never a shortage of sunshine. In winter the sun shines for an average of 6.32 hours and around 9.85 hours in the summer time. That is why they say there are only two seasons in Malta: summer and 'not-so-summer'. In actual fact, the weather is consistently so sunny and dry that a lesser vintage is caused by lack of water.

Winters are short and mild, giving the vines just enough time to rest. Fog, hail and frost are a phenomenon rarely witnessed in Malta and yields are relatively stable from vintage to vintage. Although the Maltese winters can be wet, the vines don't risk becoming waterlogged since its quartzite, red-orange soil covering the hard, but porous rock beneath is only a few spades deep. Most of the time, the Maltese countryside has a sun-baked, scorched appearance.

DEFINING MALTA

# Water Anyone?

Man will never learn to control the weather, just as he cannot master the sea, but thankfully, there are ways in which the adverse effects of the elements can be alleviated.

In Malta, rain only falls for short periods of time, averaging about 533 mm in a whole year. The rainfall on the Islands is extremely erratic and is characterized by intense, brief thunderstorms and the high billowing clouds that are a familiar sight during the winter.
In a few minutes' journey by car, one may drive from a village under flash flood to another hamlet that's enjoying bright sunshine.

The average temperature varies between 14 and 16°C from November to April and around 23°C from May to October. The hottest period is from mid-July to mid-September when the quicksilver settles between 30 and 40°C, but the hot summer days and nights are tempered by cool breezes from the surrounding sea.

Given the high temperatures and evatranspiration rates that prevail during the growing season, water stress in the vineyards is incredibly high. A vine needs to absorb considerable amounts of water over the year, normally a minimum of 700 mm of rain, which is more than the annual average in Malta.

Although the vineyards do not need to have access to water all year round, supplementary irrigation of vines during critical periods is a necessity for quality grape growing: for example, during the first two summer months after planting and at certain times during the growing season. It is only the mature vines of indigenous grape varieties that seem to cope without supplementary irrigation.

On the rare, deeper soils of fairly good texture, the rainfall is sufficient to produce adequate crops. It is the occasional year of very low rainfall that risks reducing yields drastically. Supplementary water for irrigation, usually via ground-level drip-tubes, is needed to make up for deficits and to guarantee top-quality grapes.

The quality of the water supply is considered to be a concern too. People with their gum boots in the fields have repeatedly called upon the government to come up with a policy to ensure the availability of adequate-quality water. There is need for more investment in water purification systems to enable unproductive land to be irrigated.

The climate is well suited to ripen both the late- and the early-ripening varieties. Chardonnay and Sauvignon Blanc, as well as varieties destined for sparkling wine, are picked weeks ahead of the red and later-ripening varieties such as Merlot and Cabernet, whose tannins and deep red colour are highly desirable.

In Malta, the first grapes are usually harvested in the first or second week of August. The picking of the international grape varieties is followed by the

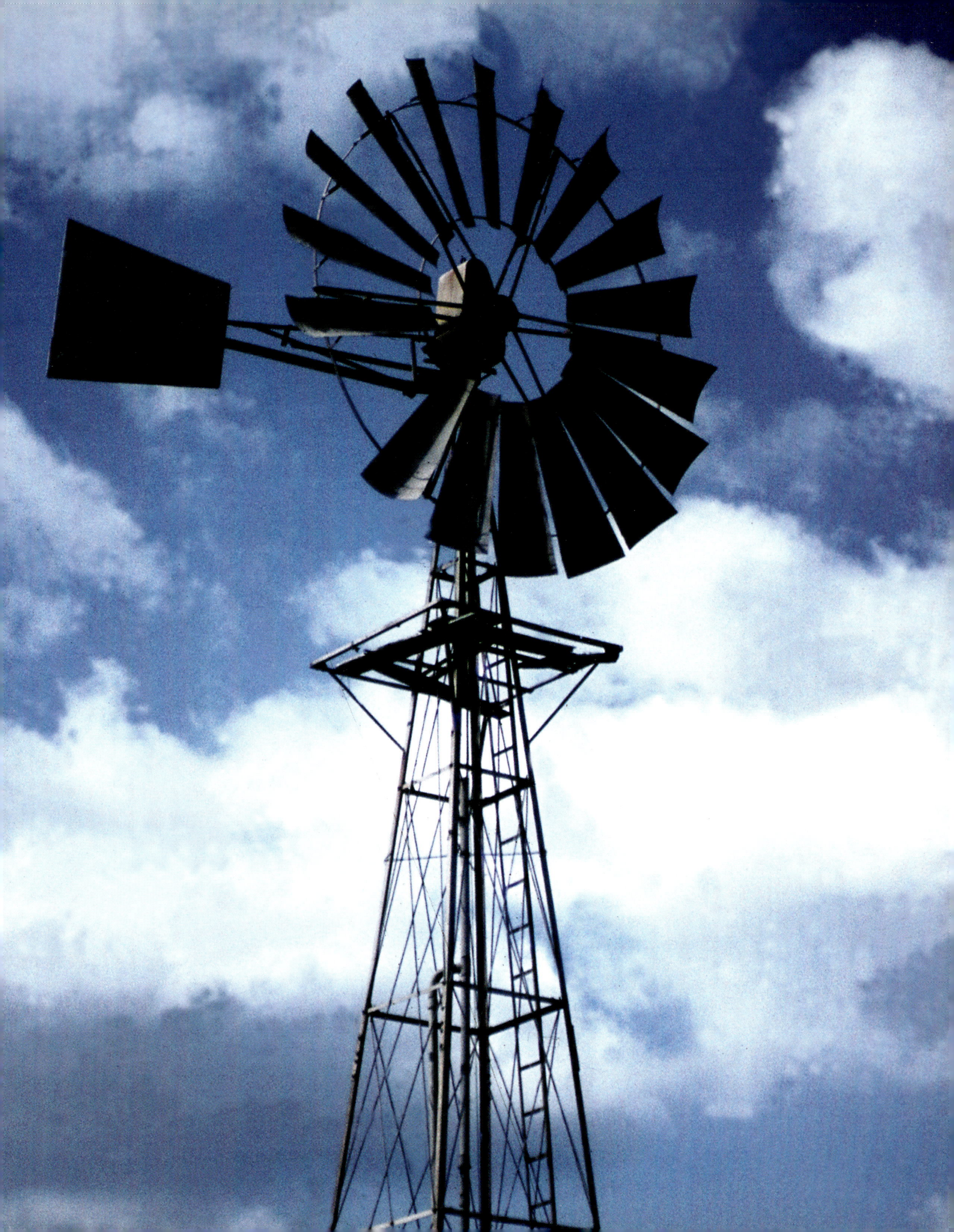

harvesting of the later-ripening indigenous varieties, the white Girgentina first and then the red Ġellewża, some time in early September.

The land under vine is very limited and patchy, which makes mechanical harvesting of grapes virtually impossible. But the advantage of 'pocket-sized' vineyards is that the picking – still traditionally done by hand – is manageable. Grapes are carefully collected in small crates to prevent them from premature crushing.

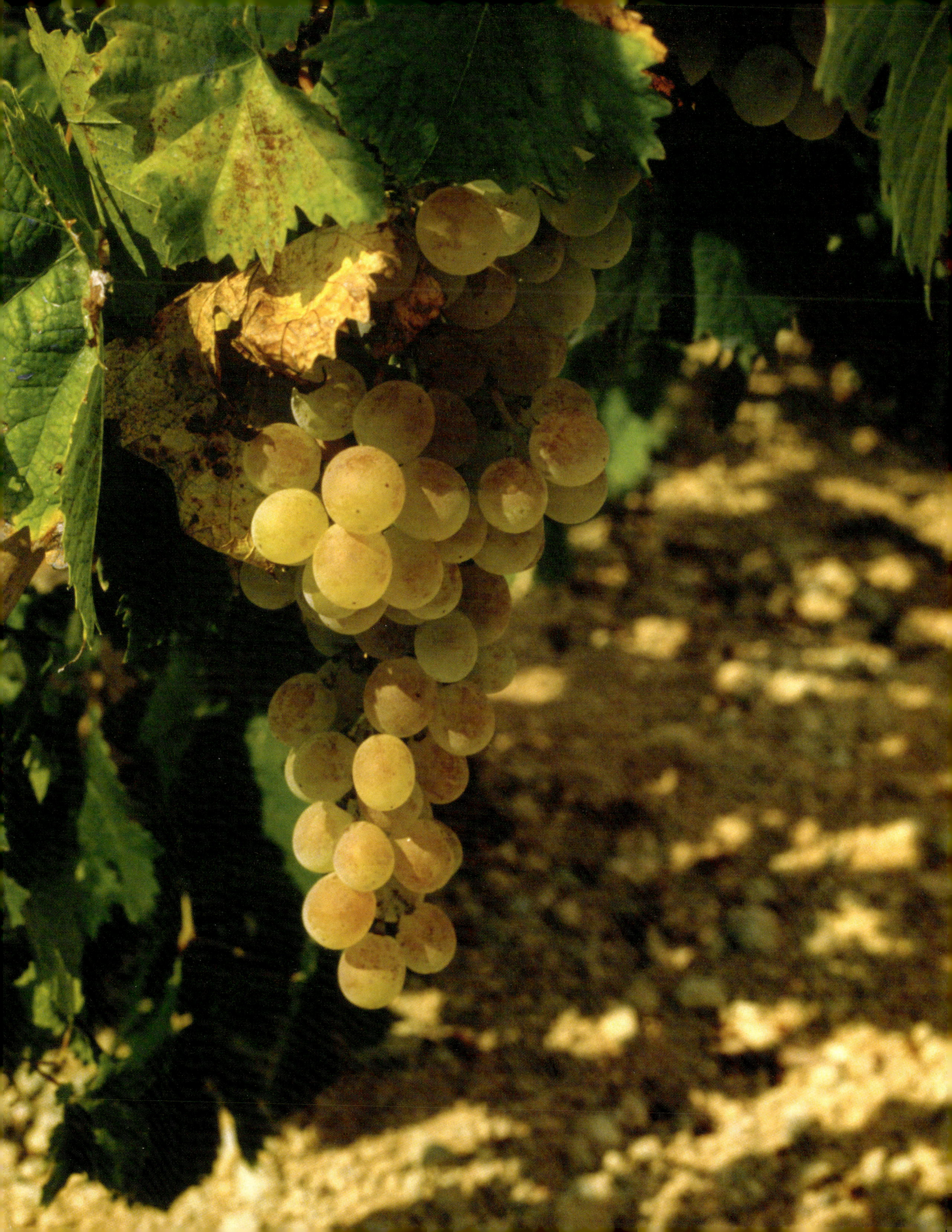

# Give Me Land...

Maybe it is hard to imagine that even here, on an archipelago hardly larger than a picnic blanket, there are a good number of different soil types to consider when planting a vineyard.

However, this is indeed the case as shown by Professor D. M. Lang who did pioneering research work in this field in 1960. Commissioned by the British government, he mapped the soils of Malta and Gozo and showed that there is significant heterogeneity in soil types and characteristics across the Islands. Different patches of land can be labelled according to the different proportions of clay, silt, sand, stones and organic matter that make up the texture of the soil.

As anywhere else, the composition of various soils will to a certain degree determine the quality of the grapes and the wine made from them. But there is no such thing as the 'one and only inimitable and ideal' soil type for growing a quality wine. By and large, the vine thrives on well-drained, poor lands of different constitution; on soils where hardly anything else can be grown. Of all the cultivated plants, the vine is the one that makes the least demands on the earth it is rooted in.

Obviously, soil characteristics will definitely influence the quality of the grapes and the wine made from them. But, in most cases the effects of soil are secondary to the capriciousness of weather and climate and all the clever human decisions a vigneron can make vis-à-vis the selection of vine varieties to be planted in his vineyard block and how to manage the vines throughout their long growing life.

Thus it would be unwise to simply correlate vine performance with the soil type as charted by Lang. Besides, the old Maltese farmers' habit of carting topsoil around and the terracing of sloping land over centuries, means that soil type is something less than a fixed value in Malta.

What is needed here is a location-specific approach. Before the rootlings or new vines are planted, soil samples have to be analysed to determine the matching rootstocks, clones and grape varieties to be planted in the new vineyard.

The rootstock is the variety providing the root system of the plant to which a fruiting variety, or scion, is then grafted. Vine nurseries sell a range of different clones of each vine variety and the vigneron will opt for the most suitable one. A clone is the name of a population of vines all derived by vegetative propagation from cuttings or buds from a single 'mother vine' by deliberate selection in nurseries.

Planting is usually carried out in the winter months January and February. The density of the planting might vary slightly, but usually the ratio is 5000 young vines per hectare. The whole art of growing quality grapes rests with the skilled vigneron who is assisted by the winemaker's viticulturist.

DEFINING MALTA

Together they will decide on how to supplement the vineyard's soil wisely and on the cultivation of suitable varieties, whilst maintaining a judicious balance between vine and terrain in order to achieve a reasonable yield of grapes for the best wine possible.

Indeed, Maltese growers have choices to make. And, although they are blessed with good soils and a near-perfect climate to match, life is not easy. They face the constant threat of land developers hunting for more land to

DEFINING MALTA

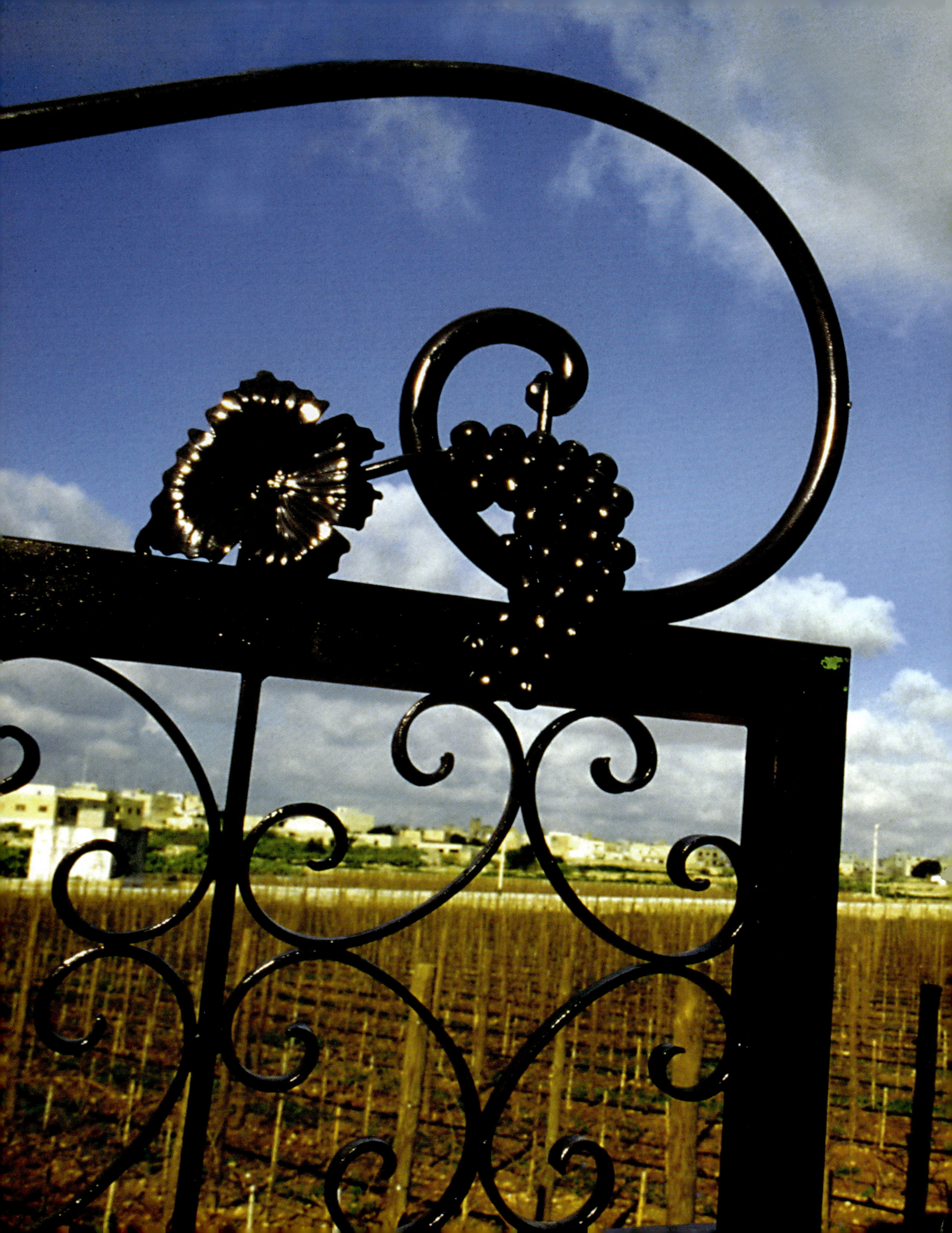

build on. Alas, the many picturesque rubble walls around the parcelled vineyards are not enough to keep the crowded town development at bay.

The building statistics are astonishing. In Malta today, there are twice as many houses and four times as much built-up area than there was just over 40 years ago. The population and the number of families has increased but definitely not doubled. It is the pressure of tourist development, property speculation and home ownership schemes that have reduced the amount of agricultural land and rural areas from a previous 135 to less than 88 square kilometres.

On the face of it, rural planning appears to be a 'palimpsest' – a manuscript re-written time and again. No land is sacred. Nonetheless, the remaining countryside is still impressive, characterised by piercing blue skies, low hills and freestone fences around tiny, terraced fields of terra-coloured soils, which are nearly all thankfully suitable for viticulture.

To the Maltese people the urge to make wine is almost genetically ingrained and will continue, even if the hardworking rural lifestyle is challenged. Clearly, the Maltese Islands are unlike any others, and neither is the country's long history of viticulture and winemaking.

# Looking Back

The recent and fundamental changes that have taken place in the vineyard and in the cellar over the last decennia are absolutely remarkable, especially against the backdrop of the long account of grape growing and winemaking in Malta.

# Merry Field Blends

Probably from the earliest times, there has been a very huge assortment of grape varieties grown in the Maltese Islands. Arguably, for a long time most of the grape varieties in existence were those brought to the country from the Eastern Mediterranean and from the hot and dry regions of Northern Africa.

Its central position on ancient trade routes in the Mediterranean Sea links the archipelago with the major grape growing countries of the world: Italy, France and Spain. As things go, a handful of cuttings would find its way to Malta, maybe as a souvenir from travels and adventures overseas.
This year some of this, a touch of that the year after, no questions asked.
Even travelling friends would bring some vine cuttings along, all in exchange for a share of the grower's potent propellant perhaps.
Who really knows?

One thing is for sure, though. At the times of the Knights of St. John of Jerusalem in the late 16th century, when winemaking revived somewhat, an impressive number of grape varieties co-existed in one and the same vineyard that seldom was much larger than a decent sized back garden.

This was the time when life was a hazardous affair and one had to provide basically everything for oneself. In a tiny plot of land livestock would run loose in a 'promiscuous' vineyard where the vines would bed down with vegetables and the olive and fruit trees.

Different grape varieties would grow together in one miniscule block of a mixed-culture vineyard and therefore all the different grapes would be harvested collectively and vinified together in one go into one wine.

The use of field blending of many and often unidentified grape varieties – versus the modern ways of vineyard management – is now looked upon as the difference between chaos and order, right brain and left brain, chance and science, intuition and reason.

Field blending was common practice for a long time. It was a way of life; a way of doing things that harks back to ancient winemaking times. It remained standard practice up to the early 20th century in Malta and even in some parts of the Old World, where winemakers would end up with a hotchpotch of flavours by mixing several grape varieties before fermenting them.

The vineyard plots would have looked nothing like the meticulous rows of vineyards planted with just one variety at a time as seen today. Over a period of centuries, a merry field blend of a whole array of unidentified varieties became adapted to the Maltese soils and climate. Together with the two indigenous varieties that today are recognized as Girgentina and Ġellewża, numerous other unidentified white and red grapes made up the base of raw material for unpretentious, commonplace amber and pitch-black wines.

In the beginning of the 1900s, the first attempt was made to index all the different grape varieties planted in Malta and Gozo. Although he was not a professional ampelographer, researcher John Borg identified a few dozen native varieties that had originated as chance seedlings and a larger number of popular Italian varieties that had been imported during the second half of the nineteenth century.

Painstakingly, he observed and recorded more than one hundred different table and wine grape varieties. By the time professor John Borg was ready to make his findings public, the vine's most fearsome enemy had arrived.

Phylloxera had come to Malta. Nearly all the varieties were destroyed in less time than poor Borg had taken to list them. Shockingly, less than a dozen varieties would survive the devastation caused by the louse, amongst which are the Girgentina and Ġellewża.

LOOKING BACK

# On the Wings of Phylloxera

Of course, it wasn't just the Maltese vineyards that were destroyed. Nearly all vitis vinifera vines in the European wine-producing countries were killed off by the phylloxera aphid, which made its way from France down south, throughout mainland Italy and the Italian islands in the second half of the 19th century.

In the Maltese Islands, the phylloxera louse was observed later, probably in June 1919, in numerous vineyards in Gozo. The agricultural district between Ramla, Xaghra and Marsalforn was particularly affected, but the initial infection must have started at least five years earlier. A year later, the insect also began destroying vineyards in Malta.

Given the fact that the prevailing winds are northwesterly, it is very plausible that the winged form of this devastating bug had been wind-borne from Sicily to land on Gozo before travelling to the main island of Malta.

Phylloxera vastatrix is an insect that lives on the vine and has a complicated life cycle, involving winged adults and burrowing larvae. It is the larvae that cause the most damage as they feed on the roots of the vine, killing it by draining the roots' sap.

The devastating insect must have spread rapidly over the Islands and weakened the vines in no time.

After all, the Maltese soil is predominantly clayish and dries out and cracks easily, giving the bug easy access to the vine's roots.

When phylloxera was discovered, the government of the time took immediate action to establish nurseries of phylloxera-resistant American vines with scions of European varieties grafted on them at Buskett in Malta and at Victoria in Gozo. Native American vines are tolerant to the aphid since they form calluses over the wounds caused by phylloxera and prevent the 'bleeding'.

At the time, Bordeaux still pretty much set the standards in vineyard husbandry – and winemaking for that matter. In reconstituting vineyards on

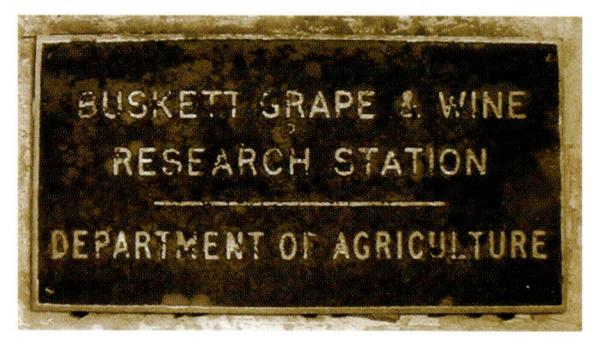

American rootstocks in the early 1920s, the Maltese farmer selected the types of rootstock that had a reputation for being vigorous, productive and tolerant to diseases and the long summer drought. By the planting season of 1923, the government had distributed 50.000 free rootlings to the growers, which reportedly was enough to meet the farmers' demand. The most commonly planted rootstock was Rupestris St George or Rupestris du Lot (as it was called in Malta at the time). This had been an early introduction to France in the fight against phylloxera, but its exact origin is unknown.

This extremely vigorous variety which enjoys a long growing season has excellent resistance to phylloxera, but the vine varieties grafted to it can easily overcrop or set poor crops, precisely because of its extreme vigour.
It is therefore no longer used for high-quality vineyards.

Nevertheless, in the years to come, the government continued growing rootstock at the national nurseries and sold the rootlings at cost price. Because there was not enough land available for rotation planting to avoid vine diseases, the authorities began to purchase rootlings from Palermo, Sicily, for a brief period of time in the 1960s. The Italian rootstock Ruggeri 140 was considered the most likely to succeed and to be the most attractive to the growers, since its characteristics resemble Rupestris St George.

At the time, the government of the day brought in expert Dr H. Olmo from the University of Davis, California, to study which grape varieties would thrive in Malta. He planted various cultivars and examined the indigenous varieties at the revamped 'Vine and Research Station' in Buskett, but his final report was never given much attention. Today, so many decennia later, the station and adjacent museum remain abandoned, but the search for the ideal grapes continues and is very much driven by the private sector although the Maltese authorities show new signs of interest.

LOOKING BACK

# One Man's Meat...

It was on the wings of the lethal Phylloxera, and in the absence of sufficient tonnage of locally grown grapes, that Maltese wine importers built a flourishing industry. As the saying goes: 'one man's meat is another man's poison'. Records show that from 1918 to 1926 Malta imported about 100.000 hectolitres of bulk wine each year for a population of about 170.000 persons.

In this day and age, modern life has no place for the heroic quantities working people used to pour down the hatch. The world's expenditure on wine has risen as consumption has fallen, of course, and the trend has been witnessed in Malta, too. Nevertheless, the figure is astonishing by comparison.

Today's wine consumption in Malta and Gozo stands at around 80.000 hectolitres per annum. That means that a smaller volume gets consumed by more than twice the amount of wine drinkers. In the 1920s only a handful of wine importers, who owned their own vessels capable of transporting large volumes, took care of this lucrative business.

One such successful company was the Coleiro Wine Company, which was established in 1898 but is no longer operational. Coleiro bought their own sailing ships and also imported grape juice from Alicante, Sicily, Crete and Cyprus to produce blended table wines such as their once popular brand 'Chevalier'. Many Maltese and Gozitan people sailed on these wine-ships.

At the time a substantial proportion of the Maltese labour force was dependent on harbour activity for gainful employment.

After World War II, Malta's First Development Plan was launched and emphasis was placed on the establishment of new local industries. Against this backdrop, the socialist Boffa government decided to convert the imported wine business to local production of wine. The government of the time insisted that farmers grow large quantities of grapes. At the same time, wine importers were somehow obliged to become wine producers and bottlers. About a total of 1,000 hectares of land were covered with vines and by 1954 the vintners of the time were pressing some 85.000 hectolitres of grape juice.

Since those days the area under vine has once more dropped significantly. During the last couple of decades the vine had to make room for the more fashionable tomatoes and potato crops. The area of land under vine today has declined to less than half its amount in the 1950s. Today, Malta aspires to become once more self-sufficient in grape growing. The industry's target is to increase the acreage to 1,000 hectares of vines planted out by 2008.

This ambitious goal seems achievable, since assistance in the form of subsidies is now forthcoming to established farmers and grape growers from the Agricultural Department and the European Union. How different the

LOOKING BACK

present situation is to the 1950s and 1960s, which in retrospect seem so much fiercer than they did then, when policemen had been posted in front of the wineries to make sure not one single berry remained unpressed.

However, it goes to show that force hardly ever succeeds. The vintages of 1956, 1957 and 1958 happened to be abundant and, apparently not all the grapes could be pressed in time. Some of the crop was left in the fields to rot. This brought about the creation of the Farmers Wine Co-operative Society in 1960 by Dr Joe Desira Buttigieg. The Co-op's task was to press and vinify the grapes for which the vintners in the private sector did not have the crushing and storage capacity.

In 1969, the farmers united in the Co-operative Society erected their winery in a not-very-appealing hangar located amid some insignificant vineyards along the busy road that swerves into Bugibba, a frenzied tourist resort. Until recently, two weathered but noticeable wooden barrels used to rest on either side of the parking lot, perhaps in a futile attempt to attract tourist coaches. Most of them, though, tend to give the place a wide berth, since there is little for the tour guide to say because there is neither any family history nor historical roots to speak of.

As is the case with most co-operatives, the Farmers Wine Co-operative Society is rather an anonymous affair, originally inspired by lofty socialist ideas that are now old-hat. On the face of it, the Co-operative is ill-equipped to compete in today's world and as with so many others abroad, it appears to have been little more than a huge grape-crushing machine, accepting practically everything the members threw at it and fermenting the juice with no particular market in mind.

Unfortunately the wines at the Co-operative are still produced in a vacuum, cut off from the modern wine drinker's tastes. Nowadays, most farmer-members grow only nominal quantities of grapes and have their crop crushed together with the produce of other registrant-vignerons, all finally mounting to litres of unpretentious white and red farmer's wine. It remains to be seen if the Farmers Wine Co-operative will at some point turn itself into a business-like operation. Time will tell.

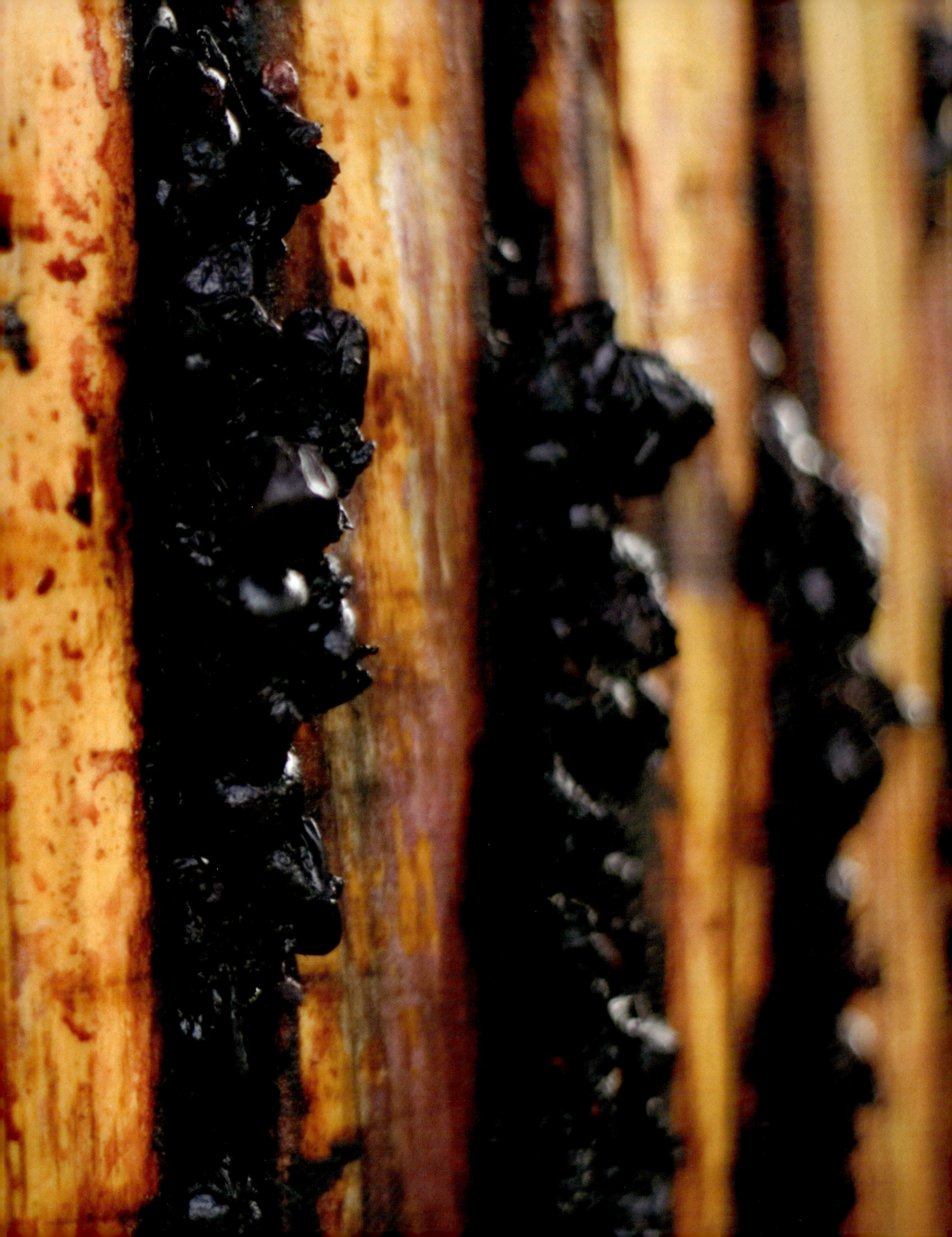

# How It Was...

Malta's leading winemakers, on the other hand, are fighting tooth and nail to dispel the old 'farmers' image of Maltese wines. And, yes, there are now some very drinkable and enjoyable 'new-wave' Maltese wines about. The forward-thinking vintners are reclaiming Malta's speck on the wine map, once again gaining respect abroad.

Admittedly, it took a while before winemaking in Malta was able to shake off the rustic cottage and farmhouse image that had previously stigmatised the industry. For far too long, Malta's wine trade had vegetated and was being kept alive in tiny patches of viticulture dotted around the country. But things have thoroughly changed.

During the last ten to fifteen years, Malta has been busy pulling its winemaking up by its boot strings from a state of mediocrity to one of international acclaim. Today, there are signs of local vinous pride. Maltese vintners have made enormous progress and there is no denying it. Malta's winegrowing chronicles can now speak about a success story of revival.

To appreciate what all the excitement is about, you have to look at where this tiny wine-producing island is coming from. At one time people might even have wondered whether much of the cheap wine was really made from grapes at all. Actually, until not very long ago, most Maltese wines served in restaurants and bars were of the 'homemade' type, having a reputation of being rather potent stuff, whether red or white, from either the Maltese mainland or from Gozo.

As the story goes – probably apocryphal – a founder of a small local winery lay on his deathbed and croakingly beckoned his son to approach. "Listen carefully", he whispered, "I must tell you this", as he paused to gather his last gasp, "it is also possible to make wine from grapes".

The moral for the unwary visitor to the Islands is that, long before the term 'les garagists' was coined to refer to those boutique French wine producers turning out excellent, expensive cult-wines, lesser Maltese names were busy in their garages bottling graphic but often anonymous concoctions in recycled Johnny Walker bottles. Thankfully, the cottage industry of the thousand-and-one amateur producers responsible for making the so-called 'farmer's wine' has as good as completely disappeared.

The Maltese winemaking industry has turned professional. While winemaking is now only in the hands of a few experienced and quality-driven vintners, the choice of quality wines made in Malta has increased dramatically.

The initial successes can be attributed to the introduction and clever use of up-to-date methods of vinification. At the larger wineries, expert control is maintained throughout the fermentation process that plays a critical role in the making of a glorious wine. The major players, Emmanuel Delicata and Marsovin, the leading wineries that facetiously enough are situated a stone's throw away from each other in Marsa, as well as Meridiana Wine Estate at Ta' Qali, have taken on board all the 'lessons' of modern winemaking.

As they kick up dust with their very palatable new wines on the international forum, the likes of Camilleri Wines, formerly known as Master Distributors closely follow in their tracks. The winery and tourist theme park Montekristo, which is a newly set-up business enterprise by entrepreneur Charles Polidano and his right-hand man and enfant terrible Victor Bonello, as well as a dozen of smaller licenced vintners try to catch up too.

The race for ever-increasing quality is on. Whereas it was initially perhaps the exceptional visiting flying wine consultant that administered some degree of 'shock therapy', now it seems as if Maltese wine producers hand themselves occasional repeat doses in order to stay sharp when it comes to modern winemaking techniques.
The last of the few remaining amateurs still make wine, more or less carefully and skilfully, with grapes that vary in quality. While they just wait and see how it will turn out, the major vintners have taken a completely different approach.

They are not merely taking the role of a midwife, but are the creators of a wine, controlling its making.

Technology supplies them with a range of alternatives, resulting in a vast range of different-tasting wines. The resulting wines are internationally-oriented without losing their 'Maltese-ness'.

Today's Maltese vintners are neither just industrialists nor just artists. They look at quality combined with the commercial aspect. Most wines are cleverly marketed under clear and colourful, eye-catching labels that offer the consumer an association with the warmth and passion of the Mediterranean lifestyle and Maltese heritage.

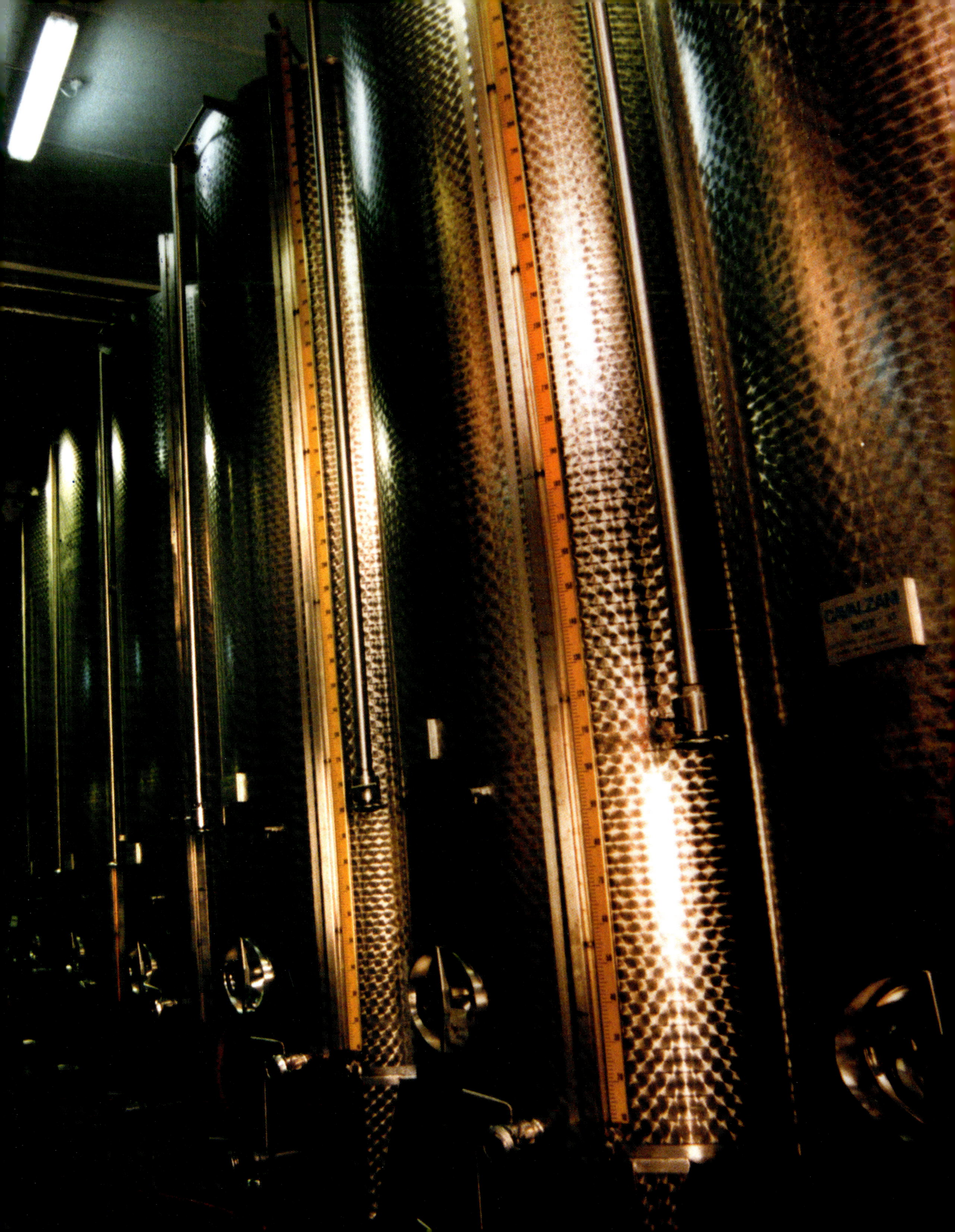

# Stepping Stones

Resourceful as they are, the Maltese winemakers have broadened their provisions to make wines that are solely made from grapes grown in Malta and really worth discussing in terms of authenticity.

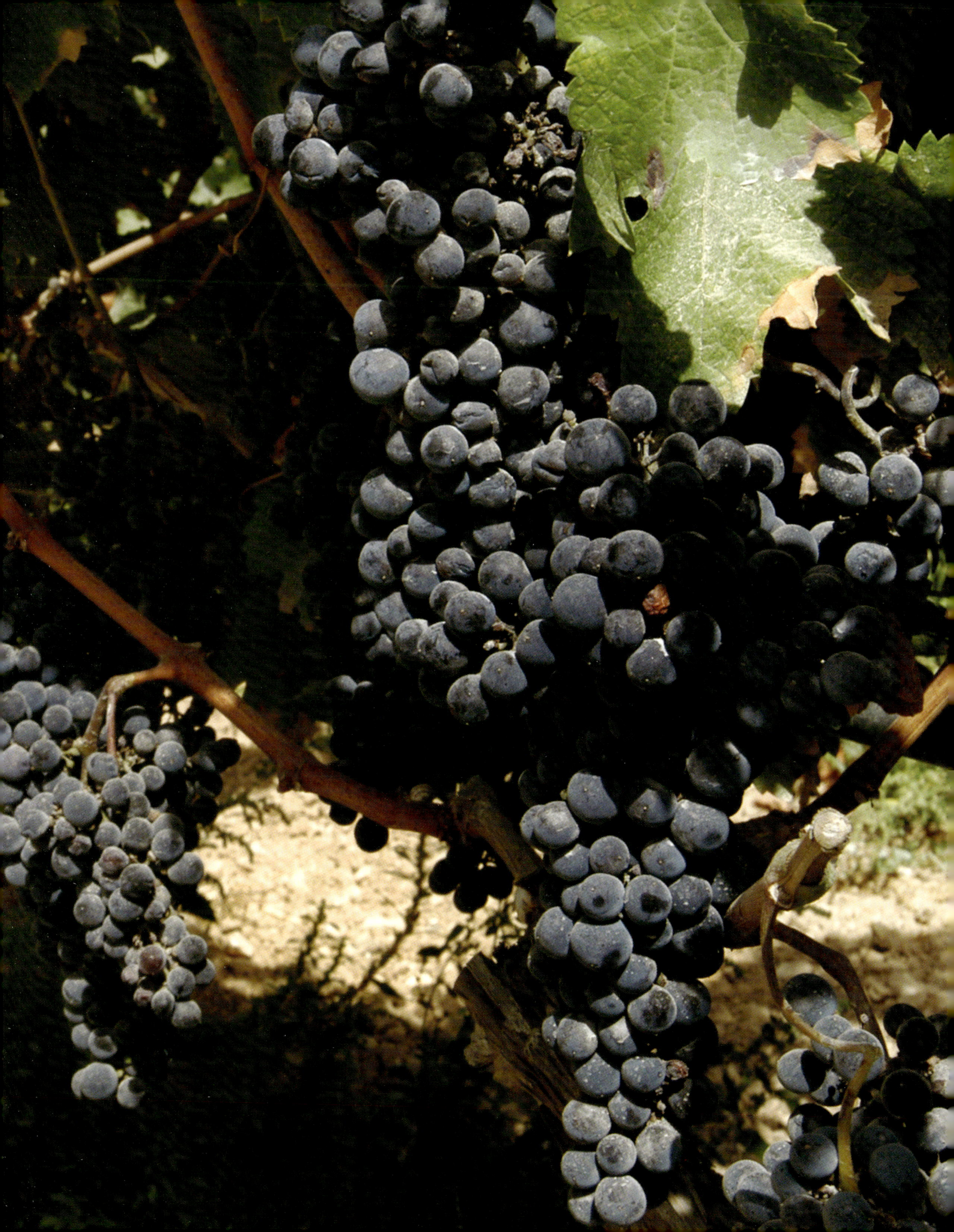

# By Means of Scarcity

The real challenge for any winemaker is to bring forth excellent wines pronouncing 'typicity'. The taste of the vintner's most expressive wines will conform to a style that is typical for wines made from grapes grown in his country's soil and climate.

Some speak of 'terroir' (basically French for soil or terrain). This is a very meaningful term in the making of a true top-drawer wine. Some maintain that a truly 'great' wine should reflect just that: the character of the farmland feeding the vines, it should embody a particular place within the countryside, the dirt itself, the subsoil beneath it and everything surrounding it.

Alas, 'terroir' is the sum of many things and wine, as life itself, is never quite that cut and dried, however. Unquestionably, in Malta, the future of winemaking lies in the fact that the Maltese vineyards and the Maltese Islands, too, certainly have their unique 'terroir'. It is just that, without any fault of their own, the island's winemakers have suffered setbacks because of the number of years it has taken them to find it, mainly due to the shortage of raw material, namely grapes.

The Census of Agriculture for 2001 revealed that the total area under vine in the Maltese Islands stood at around 500 hectares at the time, with about 450 hectares in Malta and the rest in Gozo. This area was estimated to represent a national vineyard area good for just over 1,600,000 vines that rendered a table and wine grape produce of just over 2,000,000 kilos in 2001.

At the time vineyards were concentrated mostly in the Northern District, which includes St. Paul's Bay, Mellieha and Mosta, covering an area under vine of 220 hectares. In the Western District, which comprises Rabat and Dingli, vineyards accounted for 180 hectares.

Today this is simply not a sufficient amount of Maltese acreage under vine to satisfy the increased demand for locally produced wine on the domestic market. Actually, there has been a continuous shortage of grapes to enable producers to keep pace with the increasing thirst for well-made wine that has been created by the influx of holiday makers coming from the European mainland since the 1970s.

Thankfully the Maltese people are renowned for their resourcefulness. The concept of 'lateral thinking' (a way of solving problems by rejecting traditional methods and employing unorthodox means) was not coincidentally thought up by Maltese professor and world authority of creative thinking Dr. Edward de Bono. Therefore, it should not surprise anyone that the entrepreneurial Maltese winemakers looked in the same direction the discerning, thirsty tourists started coming from.

For a long time, Maltese winemakers sourced the locally available grape varieties, mainly the white Girgentina and the black Ġellewża. But once faced with the fact that there simply weren't enough grapes available, neither the indigenous nor the international grape varieties, vintners came up with the idea of complimenting the scarcity of locally-grown native and noble varieties by trucking in fresh, often hand-picked Italian grapes.

Only in the late 1980s did the wineries actually manage to convince the Nationalist government, under the then leadership of Dr. Eddie Fenech Adami, to allow for the importation of fresh grapes to be free from duty and levies. From then onwards winemakers have been in a commercially viable position to produce wines made in Malta from grapes harvested in Italy.

Consequently, wines vinified locally have ever since been divided into two main categories according to the origin of the grapes they are made from. There are the wines made from locally-grown grapes, from either indigenous or international grape varieties, or other wines made from grapes that grow in a number of countries and which are imported.

But regardless the provenance of the grapes, commitment to quality should always begin with the selection of the grapes and is given attention at every step of the delicate process of winemaking, which explains the chilled transportation of the imported grapes in small wooden trays via refrigerated trucks.

STEPPING STONES

To date, Malta still doesn't grow the total amount of wine grapes it needs as raw material for its domestic wine market. A certain quantity, at least for the time being, needs to be imported.
The Department of Agriculture actively monitors the importation of grapes, ensuring that the grapes and grape musts that enter the country are of high quality.

As always, the final taste of the wine in question obviously depends largely on the skill of the individual Maltese winemaker whose task it is to transform bunches of grapes into a wine.

The three large wineries, Emmanuel Delicata, Marsovin and Camilleri Wines, all have been producing wines made from quality grapes harvested overseas brought in from a variety of Italian DOC regions which are often cooler grape-growing regions than Malta.
The arrival of these imported grapes has always conveniently started as the harvest in Malta finishes, thus allowing the pressing of grapes to continue for around 10 to 12 weeks between August and mid-October.

When making wine from alien grapes, the winemakers are to abide by EU labelling regulations, which require specifically that the label on the bottles of this type of wine carries the words 'Wine Produced in Malta from Grapes Harvested in Italy'.

As a rule, the protective 'spirit' of the EU law only allows a wine to be labelled as quality wine if the wine is made in the same country that the grapes were harvested in. Maltese vintners, however, have been granted permission to continue mentioning the names of the grape variety used and the vintage (or the year the grapes were harvested) on the labels of their varietal wines made from imported grapes for a limited period after succession.

This labelling issue was originally a hot potato but finally common sense prevailed with regard to the labelling issue of this type of 'Wines Made in Malta from Grapes Harvested in Italy' for sale on the domestic market only.

Actually, for some time now labels on such bottles offer a crystal-clear description and often even state the name of the particular region in Italy the grapes come from. The handpicked Merlot and Cabernet Sauvignon grapes as well as the Chardonnay, Pinot Bianco and Grigio grapes usually come from the Friuli region of north east Italy, whilst most of the Trebbiano crop is harvested in the Abruzzo region in central Italy. The Sauvignon Blanc grapes are usually sourced in Trentino and the Moscato in Piedmont in northern Italy.

# Shaping A Taste For Variety

Many who have tasted these well-made wines have often come to the conclusion that most of these single-varietal wines reflect the goodness of the grapes they are made from as good as and possibly even better than when the grapes are left in the hands of many an Italian winemaker.

The fact that a wine is made from imported grapes does not preclude that wine from being of good quality. After all, nothing 'just happens' in the winery. A fine-tasting wine is the result of deliberate decisions and constant monitoring. Being able to control temperatures to enhance or conserve fruit both before and during fermentation, optimising skin contact and extraction, managing the pomace effectively, measuring the time of fermentation and the degree of maceration afterwards, the choice of barrel or tank aging, minimising uptake of oxygen, temperature and humidity of the cellar, the type of racking regime chosen… These are a few examples of the decisions that affect the quality of the end-product for any given lot of grapes.

In the past, international wine experts, professional tasters and wine writers have been very favourable towards some of these wines and in particular towards the 'Classic Collection' of single varietal wines made by Emmanuel Delicata. Actually, Delicata have won international awards at various levels, including gold: in France (Chardonnay du Monde) and (International Challenge du Vin), Italy (Vinitaly) and the United Kingdom (International Wine Challenge).

Only but a few vociferous individuals on the local wine scene have unfairly tried to 'taint' this type of very affordable, easy drinking, likeable and correctly made wines, which have never actually made claim to the 'greatness' of some of the world's first growths. These critics should have 'placed' these wines according to the better judgment of their palates rather than by the stroke of their pen.

The reds made from Merlot or Cabernet Sauvignon, especially, have always been like the wines produced at source from the grapes in Italy, full of sappy fruit. They sit astride the frontier between unoaked light-bodied and medium-bodied reds. The fact that they are nice when drunk cellar-cool and young, and simply brimming over with young fruit character without any taste of woodiness, makes them fall very naturally into 'the lively set'.

The whites have always matched good examples of light, dry wines that reflect Italy's straw-coloured wines such as some of the best Soave and Frascati. If anything, the dry, crisp and lean whites made in Malta from Chardonnay, Sauvignon Blanc, Pinot Bianco and Pinot Grigio are not as neutral as the regional Italian versions and show a more identifiable taste of the respective grape variety.

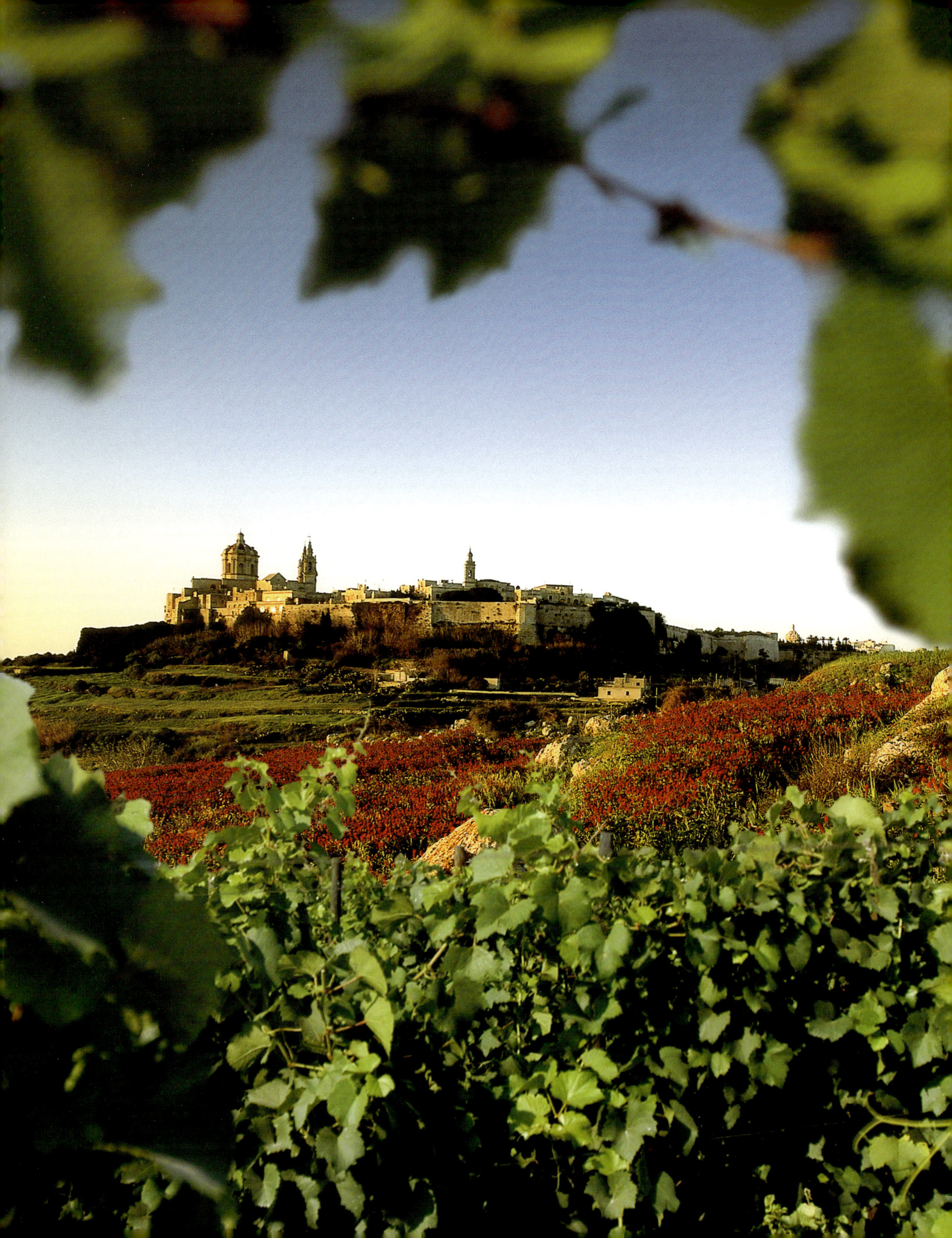

Modern winemaking techniques have constantly been applied to preserve and express the character of each individual grape variety and reflect the particular cooler local growing conditions of the region where the grapes are picked. Aptly applied technology has been used as a positive aid in reflecting and respecting each different grape variety's characteristics, rendering a recognizable wine as the final product.

Over time, these mono-varietal wines have become accepted by wine drinkers as well-made and enjoyable wines, equally comparable to imported wines sold at the same or higher price point. They have always appealed to palate and pocket. Any other distinctions, although possibly important, were always really secondary – most definitely from the consumer's point of view.

The reality is that these affordable wines made from one single grape variety have weaned the Maltese (wine) drinker on to better-made wine. It's the wines made from alien grapes that have gradually shaped the domestic demand for wine that can sustain the Maltese wine industry and upcoming viticultural development plan – albeit until recently protected by restrictive government levies on imported wines. They will probably not be around for ever since luckily enough more and more locally grown grapes become available as a replacement for the imported ones.

In fact, the interest of vintners in the wines made from imported grapes is broadened to these wines' ability to provide a solid financial foundation for the other bottlings that are solely made from grapes grown in Malta and which are really worth discussing in terms of authenticity.

In other words, examples like Delicata's Classic Collection, Marsovin's Varietals and Camilleri's Palatino Range have been successful means to an end. Imported Italian grapes have substituted the shortage of locally available grape varieties. The sales of the resulting single varietal wines in the Maltese marketplace have been providing in part the initial capital investment that was needed to finish the upgrade of cellar technology and winery facilities as well as the rationale to plant new vineyards.

# Viticultural Revival

After little more than a decade of planting international grape varieties, the first mature generation of what is called 'Malta Grown Wines' is capturing the limelight.

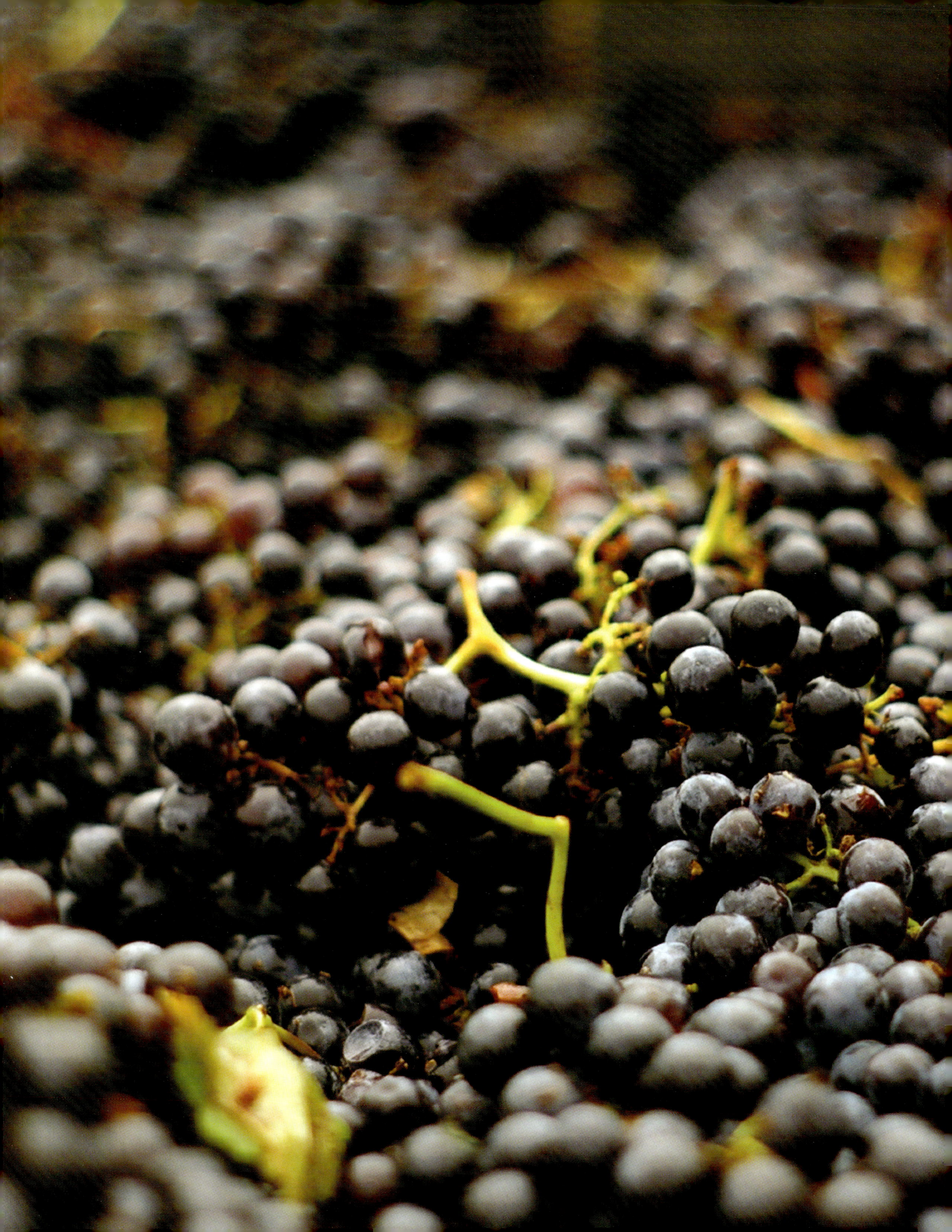

# Goodness Grapes Me!

One of the most encouraging changes in bantam Malta during the last ten years is indeed the winegrowers' increasing persistence and commitment to the viticultural development. Where land for vines is anything but abundant, they are still managing to cultivate several vitis vinifera whose names were relatively unknown to the Maltese consumer.

Nearly all wines consumed worldwide come from the wine vine 'vitis vinifera'. The origins of vitis vinifera are unclear but it is believed that this family of vines evolved over many millennia from the wild vines that thrived in Central Asia. Over this long period thousands of recognisably distinct varieties of wine producing grapes have evolved. Each variety has its own characteristics and properties that enable it to play its part in the production of wine in some part of the world. Some vitis vinifera have become so popular and so widespread in many winemaking countries that they have been dubbed 'international varieties'. Other grape varieties remained firmly rooted and did not leave their native country. These varieties are unique and called indigenous or native grape varieties.

Till recently, Maltese winemakers only had two main grape varieties with which to produce Maltese wine: the two indigenous grape varieties Girgentina and Ġellewża. Of late, new international grape varieties have been planted using modern viticultural techniques.

Rarely before has so much activity taken place in the Maltese vineyard as it has today. An assortment of international varieties such as Chardonnay, Sauvignon Blanc, Viognier, Pinot Blanc, Moscato, Grenache, Carignan, Merlot, Petit Verdot, Cabernet Sauvignon and Franc, Tempranillo, Sangiovese and Syrah vines already triumphs in places where no other crops can be grown.

Not only have these international grape varieties of selected French and Italian clones on American rootstock found a place in Malta. There are also exciting experiments ongoing in small, delimited estates where creative vignerons have grafted certain red grape varieties such as Nero d'Avola onto the phylloxera-resistant old vines of Girgentina and Ġellewża in the goblet-trained or bush method.

The search for better and more typical Malta grown wines is moving away from the cellar more than ever and focuses on the intrinsic properties of the land feeding the vines.

Because the forward-thinking vintners have invested heavily to get their woodhouse in order, they have found themselves in a better position to rush into the countryside to plant even more vineyards. Moreover, en route, they have also changed their thinking from a 'laissez pousser' attitude to a philosophy of modern vineyard husbandry.

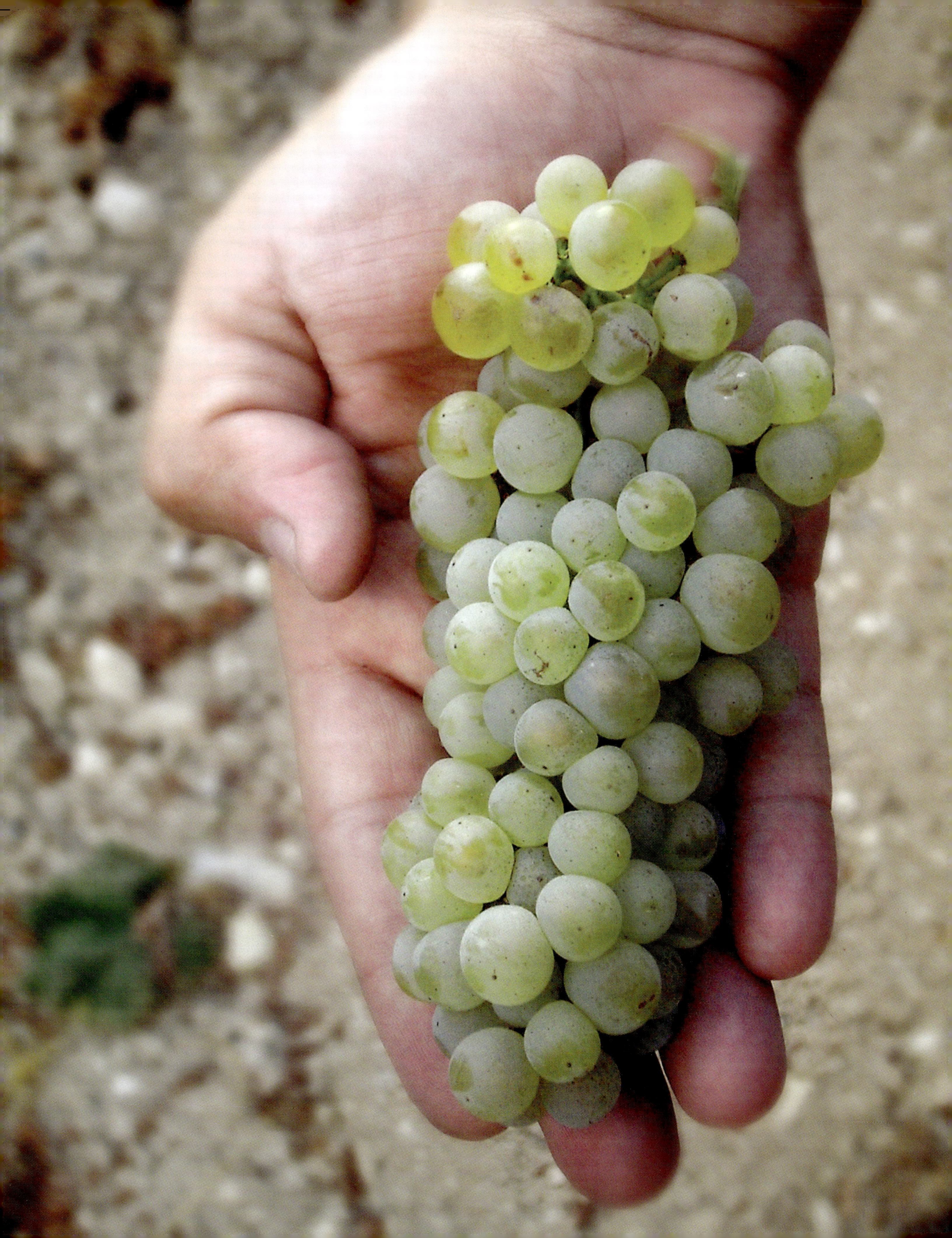

The first significant step towards the production of good Maltese wines dates back to the late 1970s when Marsovin tried their hand at the cultivation and vinification of international grape varieties such as Cabernet Sauvignon or Ruby Cabernet. But international grape varieties have only really found their roots going into Maltese soil during the last ten or fifteen years, a trend that has been witnessed in other wine producing regions in the Mediterranean as well.

In the running up to full European membership, in one of the very few EU countries where there simply is not yet enough land under vine, it was pretty much up to the 'Malta Wines & Vines Association' (a body made up by the majority of winemakers) to do most of the lobbying to get more land under vine. Although the EU has a general ban on the planting of new vineyards until 2010, tiny, new member-state Malta has meanwhile been given the green light by the EU and has obtained a concession to plant more vines. Besides the romantic appeal of operating one's own vineyard, the government and EU subsidies temporarily forthcoming are a big help, even in enticing more people with access to land to grow international grape varieties. Another important factor for the aspirant grape growers to consider is that the demand for grapes is already there. The winemakers need these grapes for an existing market, not an expected one.

Considerable efforts have been made in a short time to ensure that the acreage under vine increased steadily to make Malta self-sufficient in grape growing. It will obviously take some time before the Maltese Islands are able to grow enough grapes to meet the demand for wine on the domestic market.

So, with the influx of tourists in the 70s, 80s and 90s, the Maltese vintners were faced with a more demanding market that held them to higher standards. While in the short term it was necessary to import grapes for survival, the logical long-term solution was clearly to start a general clean-up of the national vineyard, together with a more careful adaptation of grape varieties.

Change needs time, especially changes in the vineyard, where it is a much more painstaking process than the upgrading of the winery. Grubby cellars can be cleaned up overnight. The trial-and-error process is more complicated in a situation where the raw material on which to base experiments only appears once a year and when vineyard maturity takes decades.

Since the mid-1990s, the vintners' contribution to vineyard management has greatly developed, and the leading producers are concentrating on 'growing' better wine as opposed to simply 'making' better wine. When planning a new vineyard, tasks include vineyard site selection, the choosing of soil-suitable varieties and rootstocks as well as the laying out and the actual planting of the vineyard.

Throughout the year, pruning needs to be carried out to provide healthy growth for the coming harvest, the vines' leaf canopy has to be cared for to ensure good air flow and to manipulate sunlight exposure. Other chores consist of pest control to eradicate vine diseases, regulating yields and determining the precise time of the harvest. These are all significant contributing factors to overall quality.

There are a few vineyards which are still inter-planted, and a minority of farmers still harvest mixes of grape varieties in the vineyard. However, Malta has come a long way and the main vintners are not only the driving force behind the new plantings. The principal winemakers also assist the growers and impose a considerable degree of order on the vignerons that supply them with grapes. It is now even possible to begin differentiating between the distinctive expressions of a single variety planted in different areas, and then to determine which sites give the best results.

This path has only recently been forged, but already we are seeing more or less concrete and palatable results. Despite the fact that the major wineries have different ideas about vineyard management and winemaking and deliver different styles of wines, the hot climate and the rocky soils gives them a common heritage, to the point that a wine taster who is familiar with Maltese wines can recognise common characteristics in the quality wines.

As a result of their efforts, a number of Maltese wine producers are now turning out modern wines, still from indigenous grape varieties but more and more increasingly from a good dozen recently adopted international varieties.

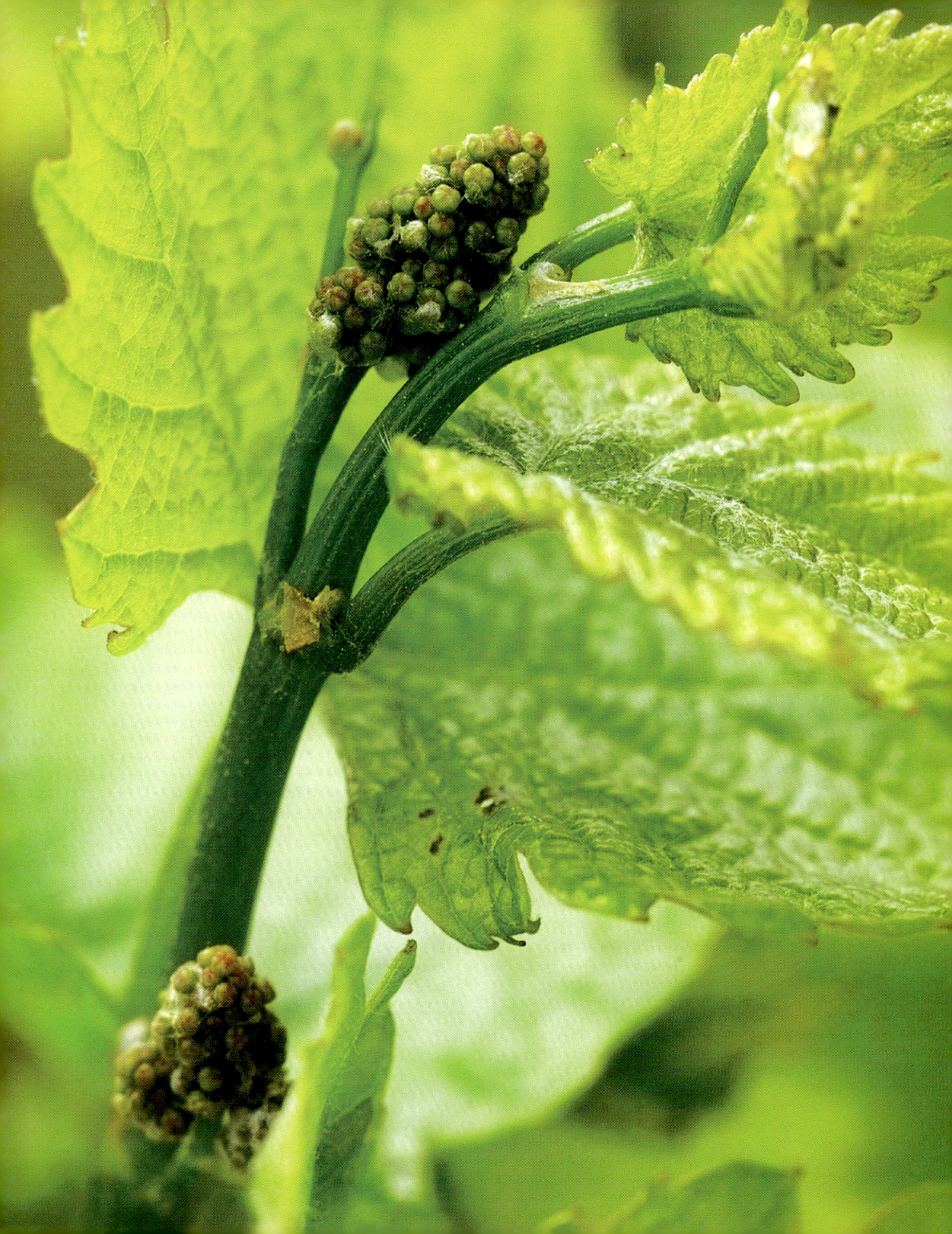

# Vines For Wines

Winemakers have moved into the vineyards and realised that the making of great wine starts precisely there. They have been frantically busy planting international grape varieties that go by names which are easy to recognise by the thirsty visitors that come on holiday to Malta and Gozo.

An example of this is the wind of change that blew through the largest wine producing company, Emmanuel Delicata. This is a family-run winery which was established in 1907 and currently has around 80 employees. New vines coupled with shrewd winemaking by managing director and third generation winemaker George Delicata are making his fruit-turboed wines acquire international acclaim by many wine critics.

Delicata's viticultural project 'Vines for Wines' resulted in the right ingredients. Winemaker George Delicata was quick to put his cellar experience to use to bring about a first generation of quality wines that embodied the beginning of a 'gout de terroir'. Examples of these are Delicata's Fior del Mondo, Medina Vineyards, Victoria Heights, Grand Vin de Hauteville and Gran Cavalier ranges. At least seventeen different white, rosé and red wines are made entirely from Malta grown grapes now that they are finally available.

Amongst Malta's other principal winemakers is Marsovin, for long spearheaded by Tony Cassar assisted by his son Jeremy Cassar, French-taught oenologist Philip Tonna and viticulturist Christian Cremona. A much smaller operation is the Meridiana Wine Estate (in which Marchese Antinori is involved) with director Mark Miceli-Farrugia at the helm. Here winemaking is in the hands of oenologist Roger Aquilina who joined after 18 years of work experience at the Farmers Wine Co-operative. Another family-run firm is Camilleri Wines directed by Louie Camilleri. They too have come a long way as far as cellar technology is concerned and have switched to Malta-grown grapes for the making of a number of wines including their Palatino range which was once solely made from imported grapes.

At these other principal wineries, modernisation is now complete, expert control is maintained throughout the entire process of vinification and capital is now being reserved for new plantations and the acquirement and upkeep of 'estates'.

In the early 1990s, mainly red varietals like those found in the Haut-Médoc and the white variety Chardonnay were planted in the Marsovin-owned vineyards, following a first pilot project with Cabernet plantings that Marsovin had embarked on in the late 1970s.

Meridiana, positioning itself as a 'boutique' winery, re-grafted most of its 91,000 vines (18 hectares) bordering the redundant RAF airstrip, to accommodate the increasing demand for reds at the higher price point. Meanwhile, Meridiana is also planning to expand by sourcing grapes from another 21 hectares of vineyards in Malta and Gozo largely tended by partnering vignerons. This should double Meridiana's total acreage and scant production.

While not owning a single vineyard itself, it is Emmanuel Delicata that controls more hectares under vine than any of the other main winemakers, thanks to its vineyard management scheme called 'Vines for Wines'.

Like other upcoming wine-producing countries, Malta is today in search of

VITICULTURAL REVIVAL

quality in the vineyard. A decade ago, for example, a visit to a winery basically involved wandering among the barrels and tanks while listening to a lecture about things to come. Things have changed in the last couple of years. The producers have had to take off their wine-stained lab coats and get their boots dirty in the vineyard.

A few years ago, Delicata installed a computerised system which maps out every single parcel of every grower – "a winemaker's dream", according to Dr. Edric Bonello, head of the viticultural and oenology department.

There is full traceability down to minute technical details. The method in place allows prediction of what the next vintage will be like, which grapes Delicata will be using for which blends, and what will give single vineyard possibilities. More importantly, the system has been instrumental in instilling a new spirit among the partnering vignerons. The old philosophy of the growers was that each member would do his own thing and grow grapes as he deemed fit.

Dr. Bonello explains: "We now have over 130 ha (or 1,200 'tumoli') under our full control. The vignerons follow our instructions regarding pest and yield control, irrigation and water management as well as when to pick, and consequently they get paid quality-related bonuses. What we are doing is converting a patchwork of vineyards into a company's domaine. With over 380 established and budding grape suppliers to deal with, this is a task that needs close monitoring by a team of dedicated experts in the field".

The move toward focusing on the vineyard has allowed the wine producers to put their house in order and to do a bit of spring-cleaning. They have learned a lot in the process.

Dr. Bonello is optimistic about recent developments. He explains that: "Over the past few years we have collected and analysed important data, especially with regards to identifying the ideal clonal selection of each and every vine variety." This vital information could easily be the make-or-break factor towards the success of a vineyard's performance. Each variety has a number of different clones and the newly gained experience in the field now permits the choice of one that will not only suit that one particular vineyard's microclimate and soil structure, but will also meet the requirements of the winemaker regarding the individual characteristics of that particular grape.

The resulting fruit shows great promise. After all, there is – and always has been – a natural place for vines in Malta. Early successes, greater self-confidence and fierce competition make Maltese wine producers ponder more and more on vines and soil.

# Championing Wines

The quest for more land under vine has been applauded on the political forum as well. The planting of vines allows millions of Maltese Liri (once equalling nearly three million Euros) to be kept within Malta's small economy, which would otherwise have been spent on imports.

Environmentalists, whether wine-loving or not, embrace the project as well. It conserves the agricultural use of land and provides attractive green-belt areas of well maintained farmland, which are so badly needed in this already over-developed, tiny island that depends for its survival on the influx of more than one million sunseekers yearly.

Yes, all credit goes to the entrepreneurial Maltese winemakers and vignerons for planting vines for wines. The sight of acres upon acres of vine-filled fields, verdant expanses dotted with the purple-red and golden colours of the fruit peeping through their mantle of leaves is one that never fails to delight.

Nonetheless, it will be consumer demand, and not Malta's pygmy green movement, that will dictate the future of Maltese wine. Reassuring though is the knowledge that, throughout the years, the Maltese wine drinkers have become more and more appreciative of good wine, and their taste buds are all set for further refinement.

The foreign wine drinkers coming to this holiday destination, too, have been trained to demand well-made wine with all its local character intact. Or, as Delicata's associate director, Bill Hermitage, puts it: "The real challenge now is not so much to put out yet another classic wine on par with its foreign counterpart, but rather to bring forth excellent new wines pronouncing Malta's typicity by championing our own Girgentina and Ġellewża grapes and by pioneering with suitable international varieties".

Strong words, indeed. Yet not surprising for a producer majoring on the not-so-local Syrah variety to excellent effect, judging by the quality of the blockbuster Gran Cavalier Syrah.

Malta's wineries search for complexity in what is essentially a hot region, to express its 'soil'. "We even vinify certain parcels of land separately to conserve microclimatic distinctions", Bill Hermitage explains. "It might be hard to argue that there actually are great differences between our 380 pocket-sized vineyards all located within the island's radius of 12 miles. Nonetheless our nose tells us that a Merlot clone in Gozo renders a meatier red wine than one vinified in the same way from grapes grown on the main island".

Not so long ago, ex-chairman of Marsovin, Tony Cassar also has been quoted saying he believes in the quest for better quality wines and has underscored the important role of the soil in the making of a wine. Whereas Delicata does not exclude the making of premium wines from grapes coming from different vineyards, Tony Cassar and his son Jeremy have been favouring the making of so-called estate wines. They are of the opinion that wines made from grapes from a single vineyard in particular incorporate the character of the variety grown on a specific parcel of land.

Marsovin have followed this path and are labelling some of their premium wines as 'Private Estate Selection Wines'. Antonin Noir and the meritage Marnisi are produced from the Marnisi Estate in Marsaxlokk, whilst another red, Grand Maitre - marketed as an expensive icon wine - comes from their Ghajn Rihana Estate.

From the Ramla l-Hamra Valley Estate in Gozo, which covers around four hectares, Marsovin has harvested the Chardonnay and some Pinot Bianco grapes for the award-winning Antonin Blanc. The Cheval Franc Estate yields grapes for another red, their Cheval Franc. The crops from the Wardija Estate are used for their full sparkling wine (made in the Méthode Traditionelle) called Cassar De Malte.

Generally, these wineries agree that the specific climate and soil here are different to conditions found anywhere else in the Mediterranean. But while Delicata resolutely advocate the championing of all suitable grapes, especially the traditional, bush-grown Girgentina and Ġellewża varieties, Meridiana Wine Estate, on the other hand, dismiss a priori the use of these native grapes, which are allegedly too low in natural sugars and acidity.

Marsovin and Camilleri Wines have reluctantly come round to the idea of using the indigenous varieties too, but it appears that they value them less, judging by the sparse mentioning the Girgentina and Ġellewża varieties have been getting in their wine portfolios.

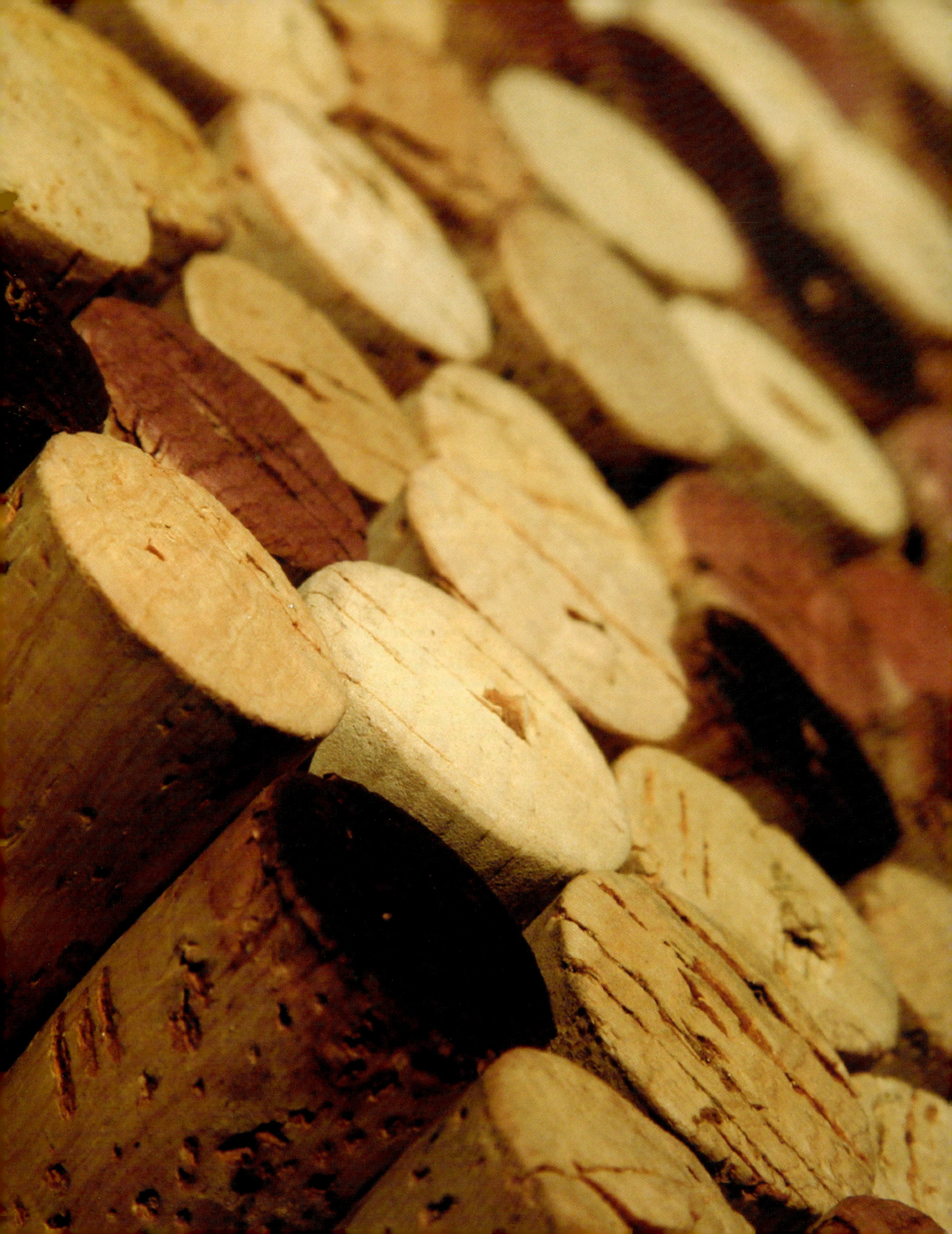

# Fostering Quality

Maltese wines need to be fostered and the lawmaker also has a role to play in assuring wine drinkers get quality from the vineyard to the table.

# You, The Consumer

Nature is not the sole factor in determining the quality of wine. The creation of quality wine is the result of careful grape growing (viticulture), and skilful winemaking (vinification), the conversion of grapes into wine. Viticulture and vinification are complementary. Neither is more important. 'Winegrowing' is the best possible term to refer to the entire process whereby the vigneron is committed to growing the best possible grapes from his vineyard as raw material for the winemaker who is devoted to the making of the best possible wine from those grapes.

Besides the vignerons and the vintners, the country's government also has a vital role to play in improving the standards that are strengthening the true revival of Maltese wines.

To begin with, the authorities of European Union member-state Malta have to ensure that those wine laws common to all EU countries are adhered to. Like in other wine producing countries, the Maltese lawmakers need to pass certain laws and regulations that are country specific and provide for further control.

In Malta, the national Wine Act of 2002 regulates the production, importation, marketing and advertising of wine in Malta. This new Wine Act is (as are all EU member-states national wine laws) based on the principle of the fundamental EU wine law, which categorises a wine as: a table wine, a wine from an intermediate level, or a quality wine that may be labelled as a Quality Wine Produced in a Specific Region (QWPSR).

Most countries have their own translation of QWPSR and national scheme to classify wines according to specific production requirements and the provenance of the grapes they are made from. Often (abbreviated) designations such as 'Appellation Contrôlée' (AC) in France and 'Denominazione di Origine Controllata' (DOC) and superior 'Denominazione di Origine Controllata Guarantita' (DOCG) in Italy, rubberstamp a quality wine and make it carry more commercial pulling power.

Although neither designation system really guarantees the quality of the liquid in the bottle, the AC or DOC(G) endorsement at least guarantees the consumer a wine's geographical provenance, its varietal make-up and certain details of production such as yield of grapes per hectare, percentage of wine per given weight of grapes, minimum sugar (grape) and alcohol (wine) levels, minimum acidity, and possibly length of ageing.

Maltese authorities are in the process of implementing their own pecking order to classify Maltese wines of 'particular reputation and worth' officially referred to as 'Denominazzjoni ta' Oriġni Kontrollata' or DOK. This system mimics the Italian quality DOC(G) system based on the Italian law of 1963 updated in

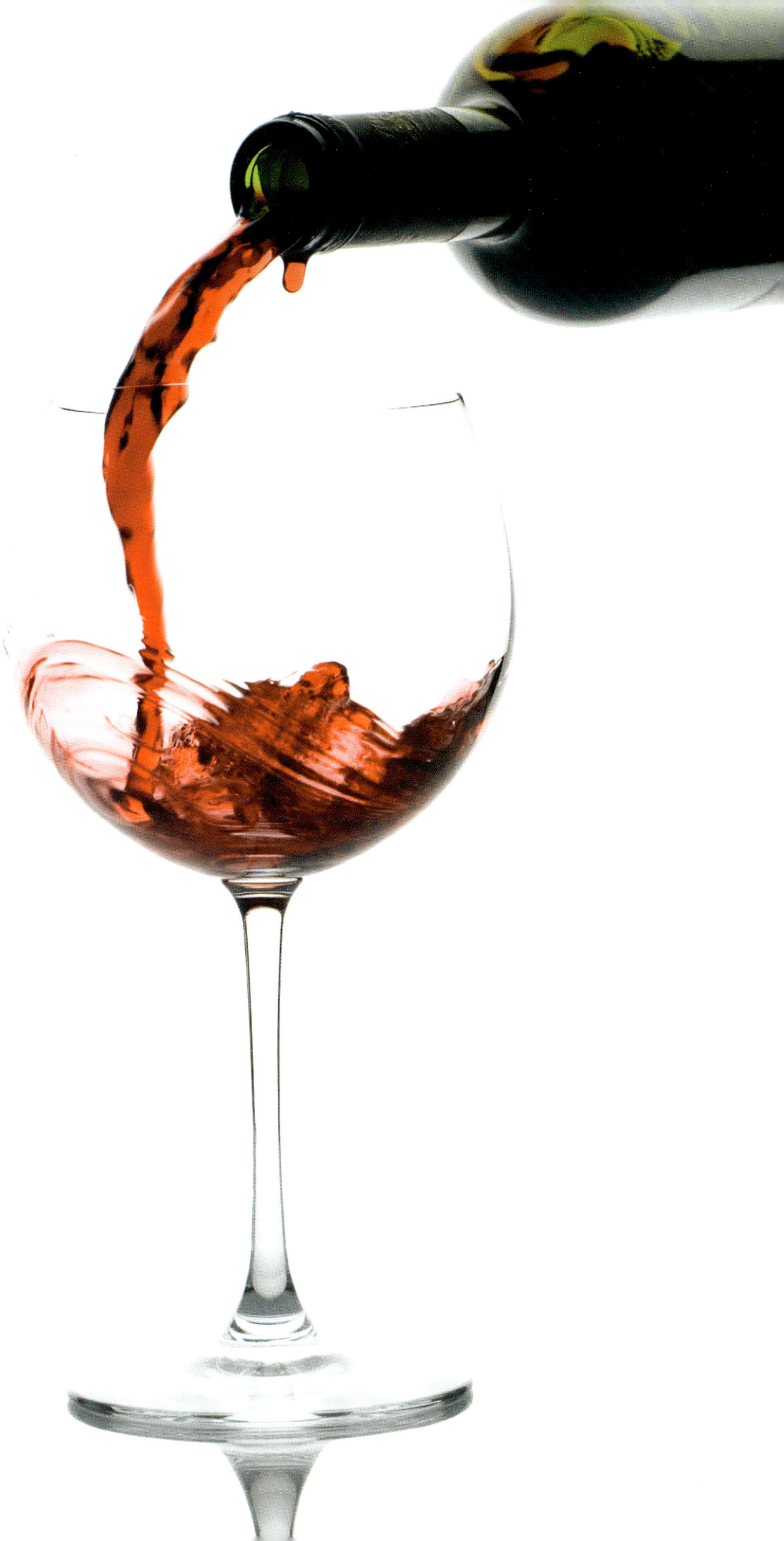

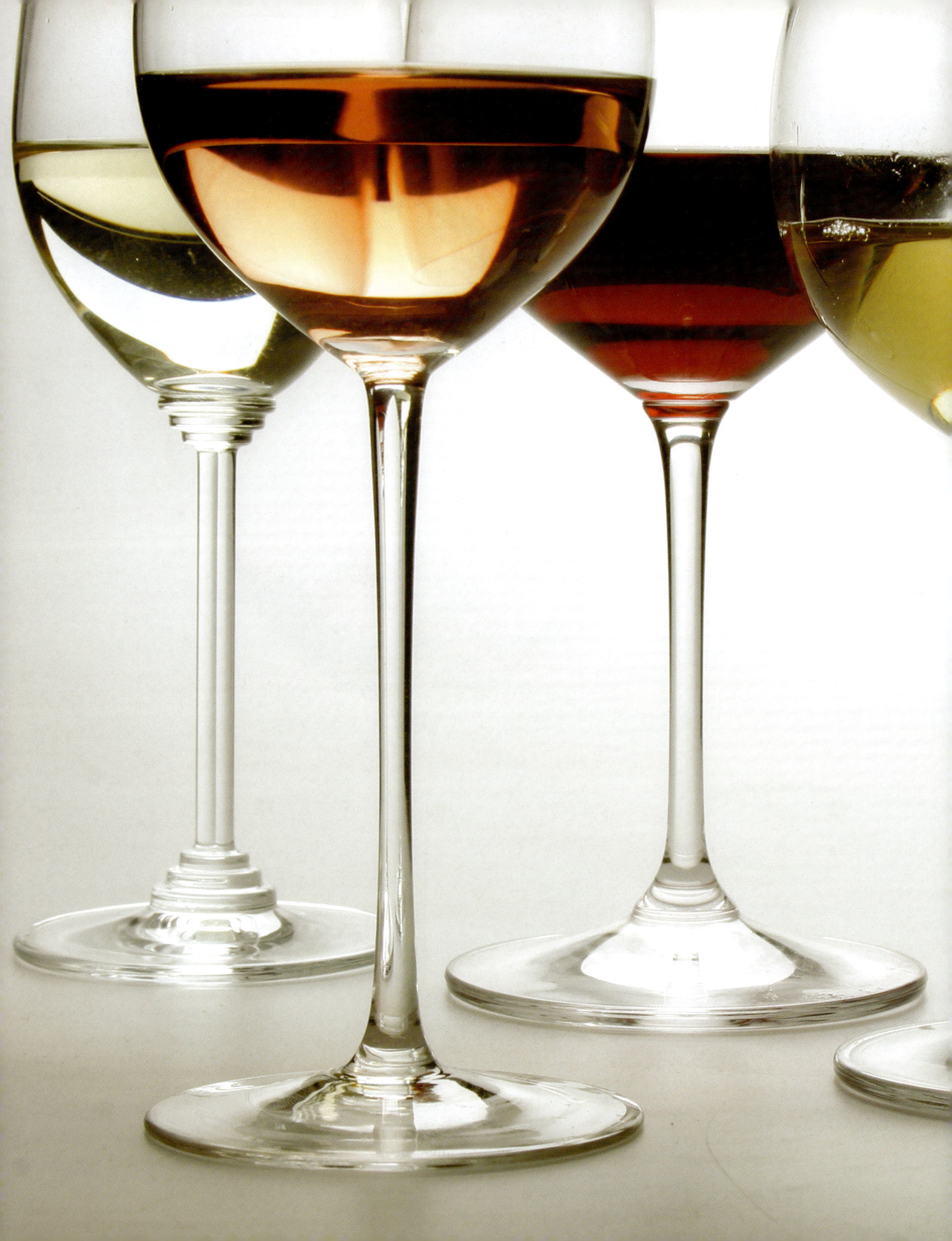

1992. DOK attempts to warrant that the location indicated on the label is indeed the origin of all grapes used in making that particular wine. Superior wines will receive a quality seal issued by the Department of Agriculture.

Endorsement by the authorities by means of a kind of standard Maltese appellation system that charts appellations, under whatever name or guise, will help in bestowing Maltese wines with consumer trust and enticing those discerning wine imbibers who are not familiar with Maltese wines.

And, let's not forget, unlike many other wine producing countries, Malta has a ready-made home market, made up of residents as well as quality conscious tourists from all the leading consumer countries of Europe, to whom to sell its wines. There are three 'thirsty consumer' tourists for every Maltese resident in the island during the course of the tourist season.

The blueprint of the Maltese DOK system has been put forward. But, by the looks of things, just like in Italy, there is a long way to go before the earth moves enough for the final set of DOK rules to bring smiles to the faces of all the country's wine producers. However, increasing pragmatism is present on both sides and everybody seems to be aware of the lessons to be learnt from the neighbouring Italians.

The first Italian appellation laws were originally drawn up by bureaucrats to prevent fraud. Today's quality-minded Italian winemakers, who aim to make top wines, find them something of a straitjacket. That's why since the 1970s many vintners deliberately threw out the DOC rulebook and downgraded the denomination of their quality wines to the lowest category of Vino da Tavola in order to make finer, modern wines. This has given birth to the likes of the so-called 'Super Tuscans'.

Maltese authorities should be aware of the huge difficulties the Italian lawmakers have had with pulling these wines back into the official fold. They needed to broaden traditional DOC's and introduce a new higher grade of Vino da Tavola called Indicazione Geografica Tipica or IGT (comparable with the French Vin de Pays).

One of the Italian (and French) wine law's fundamental aims is to protect tradition, and this is laudable. However, one can carry tradition too far, trying to drag it back to life when it scarcely exists anymore, imposing something that only came into being a short while ago.

When introducing a similar system in Malta, one must realize that the DOC - or DOK - restrictions can strangle invention and imagination. The DOK system needs to make sense. And, since the Italian likes of Villa Antinori have chosen to sometimes drop out of the DOC to enjoy the flexibility of lesser status certification by Italian wine law, the question being begged is that vintners in Malta might come to confront similar unpalatable home truths once the DOK system is up and running.

On the whole, though, a policed DOK system plotting the developing Maltese national vineyard will help Maltese wine producers sell their wines in the international market. On the other hand, as for most European wines of genuine 'quality', the name of the producer will remain at least as important as which tier of the quality ladder it comes from.

There definitely is sufficient motivation for the Maltese producers to deliver the best quality and most appealing style of new Maltese wines. Since 1st May 2004, the day Malta became a full member of the European Union, there is no longer any protection from imported wines for local wines on the home front. They have to compete directly with cheaper wines from other EU countries that washed ashore when the protective levy system was removed. Similarly, free access to the enormous wine market in Europe is available to Malta grown wines.

However, given the marginal export quantities, for the time being, doubting Thomases will have to pack their bags and travel to sunny Malta to convince themselves of the drinkability of Maltese wines that appeal in both quality and price. However, it will not be long before more of these wines will be put on wine lists and shopshelves, not only in the home market where quality tourism is being actively encouraged, but also in the main export markets such as The Benelux, the United Kingdom, France, Ireland, Germany and Scandinavia.

Malta is fast learning that today's consumers are drinking less, but a very much better quality than they did in the past, and that wine enthusiasts are willing to pay considerably more for a good-quality bottle of Malta grown wine. This is borne out in the statistics showing the average prices paid for Maltese wines over the last five years.

The average ex-cellar price of Maltese wines has risen because a completely new range of premium Malta-grown wines has come about, thanks to the viticultural advancement. Surprisingly, perhaps, there is a definite swing back to drinking wine, and this has partially been nurtured by the interest and exposure of the better-quality Maltese wines now available on the market.

Wine consumption per capita in Malta is still low, at an estimated 17 to 20 litres per annum, but the good news for the wine producers is that the younger age groups with spending power are regaining an interest in wine.
As the move toward wine drinking gains momentum in Malta, it will be interesting to see how the influx of wine imports levels out – which would be a sure sign that the consumer excitement has also been roused by the new-wave quality wines produced at home.

It is also encouraging to witness the efforts of Maltese winemakers in maintaining quality control throughout the entire manufacturing process. Thanks to the natural preservative quality of alcohol, wine is classified as a low-risk produce in the world of food quality, health, hygiene and safety. However certain winemakers are so diligent they incorporate the principles of food safety and quality management systems such as HACCP (Hazard Analysis at Critical Control Points) into the process anyhow.

With the enactment of subsidiary legislation and financial incentives, the Department of Agriculture is actively promoting the production of high quality wine grapes for Malta grown wines, which are gaining recognition and credibility.

As mentioned earlier, a new Wine Act came into force in Malta on June 21, 2002, replacing the outdated one of 1969. As in other EU countries, this new Wine Act is in line with international wine laws, with special emphasis on EU wine regulations.

This will underscore the integrity of the Maltese wines, as will the fact that Malta has also become a member of the International Organisation of the Vine and Wine (OIV), in order to be part of the international wine scene.
The OIV is an international organisation, which currently includes around 50 member countries.

Its scope is of a scientific and technical nature, working in the field of vine and vine-based products. Its main objective is the contribution to the international harmonization of practices and norms to improve the trade conditions in the vine and wine sectors, dealing with matters of vine selection, winemaking technology and economic analysis. After a period of apprehension regarding OIV membership, Malta now actively participates in sub-committees such as the one that caters for small wine producing islands and is striving to promote local wine made from indigenous grape varieties.

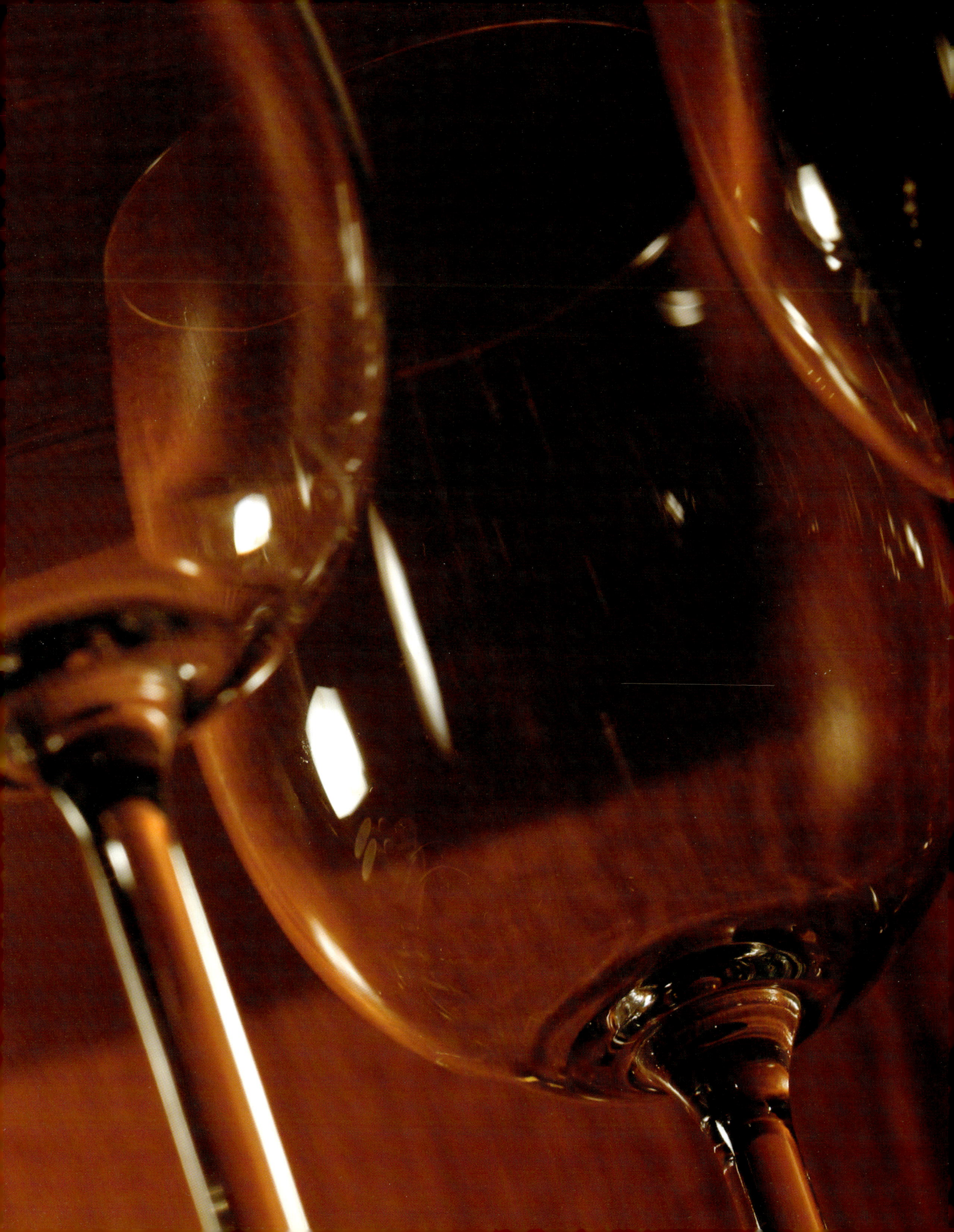

# A Grape Awakenings

For such a small pebble,
the Maltese vinescape that also
embraces native grape varieties
is wonderfully diverse.

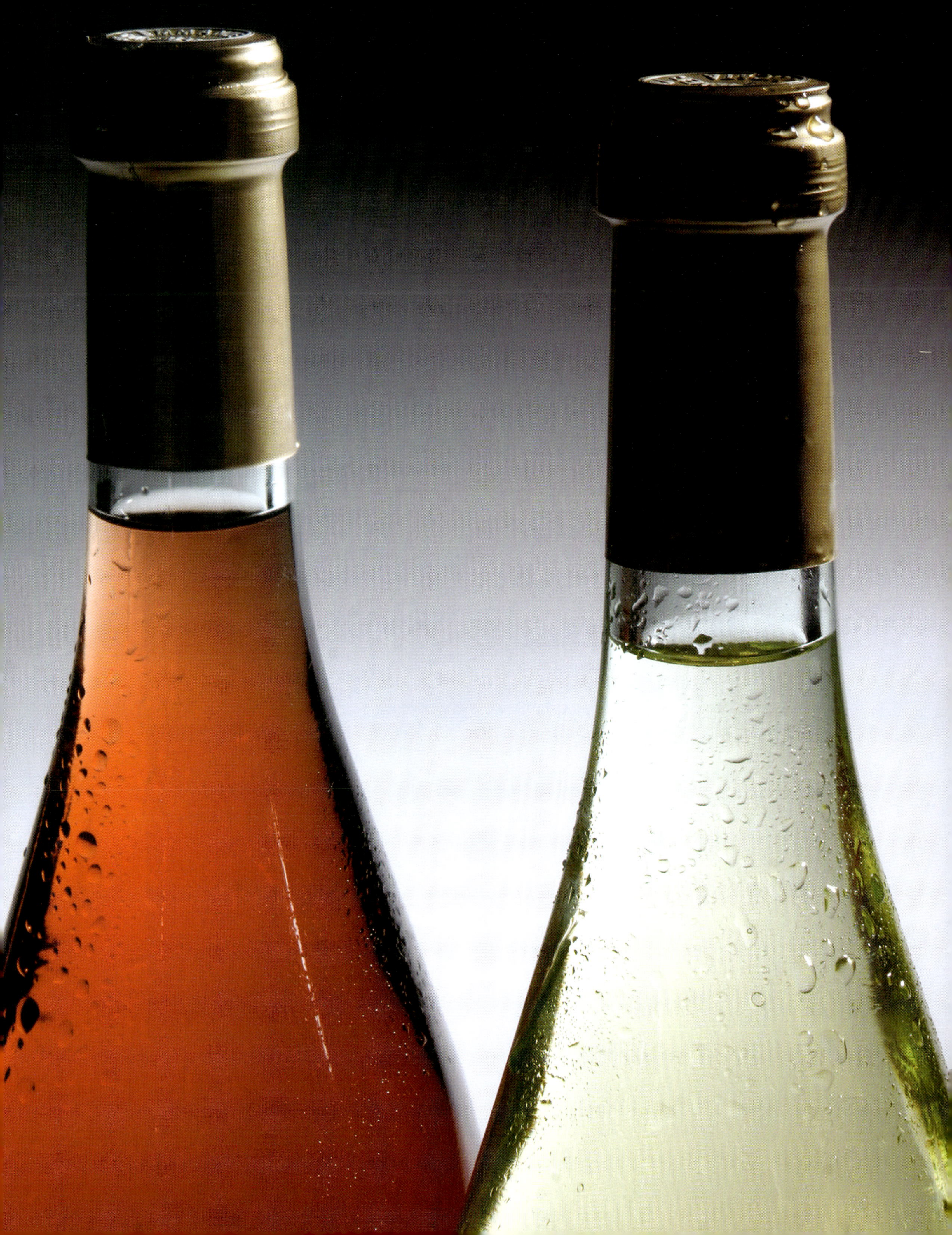

# Malta's Very Own Grapes

The previous decade of sporadic commentary on Maltese wines was mainly concerned with the virtues of two indigenous grape varieties, which can only be found in Malta, namely the Ġellewża family of black grapes, and the Girgentina, the name the white grape is known by.

The origins of Girgentina and Ġellewża are shrouded in mystery, really. Scientific research seems to indicate that neither variety is likely to be related to any other cultivar either planted in Malta or in the surrounding wine-producing areas such as Sicily or the European mainland.

No-one really knows how long they have been around in Malta, nor how they once arrived here. Some people believe the Arab rulers might have brought them along, maybe from Spain. On the other hand, it is also possible that the Girgentina and Ġellewża varieties developed locally from chance seedlings. Nobody can tell for sure.

We don't even know the origin of their names, though it has been suggested that the Maltese name Girgentina relates to the village of Girgenti in southwest Malta, where the variety was once planted in abundance. Ġellewża is the Maltese word for 'hazelnut', and the smaller grape berries are indeed very similar in shape to this nut, whilst grape berries of other varieties are usually much rounder.

At any rate, we can assume that they have been planted in Malta and Gozo for several centuries, resisting the ravages of phylloxera in the early 1920s, never slipping away farther afield, and until recently never planted in specialised vineyards. Over time these two varieties have proven their adaptability to cultivation under Maltese climatic conditions, often even without supplementary irrigation.

Girgentina and Ġellewża definitely have something going for them, otherwise wouldn't they have disappeared a long time ago? Would winemakers have stuck with them? Nonetheless, both varieties are distinctly different. Although they grow in a hot climate where grapes ripen well and their juice is rich in natural sugars, these grape varieties

GRAPE AWAKENINGS

apparently contain only enough glucose and fructose to make wines at around 9 to 10 per cent alcohol. Despite several research studies, it has not been understood why this happens. Experiments are in progress, but so far it is too early to tell what changes will help increase the natural sugar levels in these grapes.

The fact that the Maltese indigenous grape varieties are naturally low in sugar content is not in itself problematic. A grape with low sugar levels can still render a very palatable wine indeed. Normally, such a wine will remain relatively low in alcoholic strength, as there is little sugar to be converted into alcohol during the process of fermentation.

But the winemaker can intervene by means of chaptalisation, which is (in France and Germany especially) the commonplace practice of adding sucrose to grape must to enrich it and make the resulting wine stronger in alcoholic content. The EU has acknowledged the special characteristics of the indigenous Maltese varieties and thus granted permission to chaptalize an extra 1% until 2008, even though this is exceptional for wine-producing regions in warm climates.

Hopefully this will give Maltese vignerons and winemakers the time and insights required to overcome what is merely a technical problem. None of the two indigenous varieties, neither Girgentina nor Ġellewża, have enjoyed the extensive research programmes that have been applied to international varieties in the world. In light of this fact, only a few years ago this matter got some serious consideration from the Maltese government.

Unfortunately, the jury of experts (financed by an EU twinning project between Italy and Malta) that will interpret the raw data of the DNA analysis is still out. At the moment there is little, or no option in terms of choice of clones. Nobody knows which particular clone, or which group of vines shaped from one cutting selected for one particular attribute (such as the trait to produce grapes that have a natural high grape sugar level) is best.

Work and scientific research are underway, but no conclusion has emerged yet. The first indications as to which the best clones are for the native Girgentina and Ġellewża in terms of productivity, resistance to disease and insects, and natural sugar production need to be identified soon. These answers will be invaluable to those who will consider growing Girgentina and Ġellewża in the years ahead.

Hopefully things work out quickly. After all, the world wine market shows a growing interest in traditional, indigenous varieties. With today's modern approach to winemaking and viticultural attention to native grapes, the Maltese winemakers who support the indigenous Maltese grape varieties are producing wines that offer an appealing balance between innovation and authenticity. It will be interesting to see how the styles of these wines will be developed even further to please the palate of today's discerning wine enthusiasts.

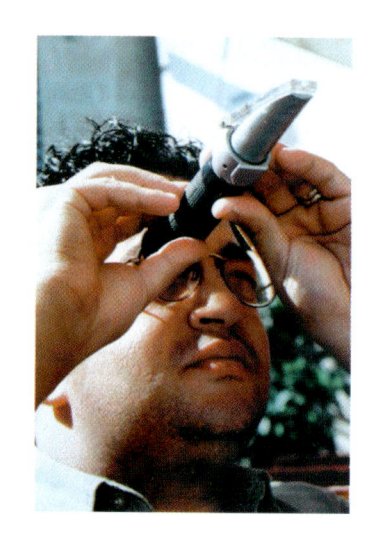

# The G-force: Ġellewża and Girgentina

Apart from an enigmatic 'food-friendly' quality, the Malta grown wines made from the indigenous varieties seem to have a dual appeal of being easy to drink as well as offering good value-for-money to the consumer.

Perhaps that is why, most of the time, the names of both grape varieties cross one's lips in the same breath. However these varieties do not strictly speaking belong to the same family, which becomes all the more of a curious fact when considering the constituents of both varieties with regards to winemaking.

ĠELLEWŻA is a red grape variety that is less pliable for the making of red wines than it is for rosés. When making a red wine from this red-skinned berry, the key is to minimize the astringent impression on the palate made by the predominantly tough tannins (which reside in the grape skin as well as in the pips and stems) while enhancing the mouthfeel.

The secret of success with Ġellewża when making a red wine is to somehow find a way to weave the fewer supple tannins with the natural colour pigments, the alcohol, the acids and the fruit flavours together in a satisfying, harmonious tapestry of taste-touch-smell sensations. This, of course, is true up to a point for all red wines, but it is somewhat truer, say, more difficult to achieve when dealing with Ġellewża. The red wines tend to be light-coloured, often with an obvious blue tinge. Even those wines low in alcoholic strength never taste sticky or cloying; there is always a wealth of tannin to tease the palate and cut in with a touch of nutty bitterness. The best examples of these often cherry-flavoured dry red wines are generally speaking light-bodied in the friendly styles of Beaujolais or Bardolino made for drinking today, tomorrow or the next couple of months.

When vinified well, with never more than a background whisper of oak (if that), even a featherweight-bodied stand alone red example of Ġellewża will surprise with a nose of boiled candy overlaid on a perfume reminiscent of the scent of violets. This is also the trait of the more serious red grape variety Mammolo, at home in central Italy and a permitted ingredient in Chianti but relatively rare today.

Perhaps the brisk tannins found in the grape skins does indeed complicate matters. Seemingly, during vinification they may put the brakes on the clean expression of the buckets of fruity flavours that jump out at you from the freshly-crushed grape berries during fermentation. That might explain why Ġellewża lends itself better as a grape variety to work with when wanting to make a fleshy rosé.

GRAPE AWAKENINGS

Its hallmark becomes apparent particularly when tasting the island's unique, medium-dry and deep pink 'Frizzante', a non-vintage semi-sparkling rosé made entirely from Ġellewża. It is highly recognisable by that undoubtedly juicy-fruit flavour of freshly cut strawberries, preceded by a nose of perfumed raspberry and a malty richness. That luscious 'gulpable' fruitiness derived from the Ġellewża grapes themselves is brightened up by a slight, palate-prickling stream of bubbles.

GIRGENTINA has been put to use in a much better way in recent vintages. Undoubtedly, the Maltese style of white wines made from Girgentina has improved dramatically over the last fifteen years. The wines are now pale, fresh, with delicate flavours and with a finish that is crisply refreshing.

In the past, the best examples showed a particular 'twang'. The worst were flabby and could have done with more flavour. The old style was very much in line with lesser examples of Italian dry white wines made from Inzolia, the white grape variety Girgentina might be related to. The Inzolia variety is also known as Ansonica, which is the white grape variety grown mainly in Tuscany but more so in western Sicily where it is valued as a relatively aromatic ingredient, often blended with the much more common Catarratto.

Maltese winemakers now favour an exquisitely fresh and fruity class of wines, with a delicate fragrance that expresses clear varietal character: a pre-eminently European style. When still fresh in the tank, the delicately perfumed wine impresses with a fine aromatic nose similar to the aromas

GRAPE AWAKENINGS

imparted by under-ripe Pinot Grigio or cool-climate, steely Chardonnay with subtle hints of sweet pear drops. In a polished, finished wine this quality shines through in a more lively way; some prickle pushes up a lovely fresh and slightly flowery smell that leaves an impression of green apple-pips with a frank 'attaque' and pleasant mouthfeel to it.

Like the white Garganega variety, which is the main grape variety used in Italy's Soave Classico zone, with yields kept well in check, Girgentina can produce fine, delicate whites fragrant of lemon and almonds, a quality which also gives the top examples of Soave a good name.

Somehow, today's better Girgentina based wines are made in an attractive style that hints of young traditional Hunter Semillon, which is low in alcohol at around 11 per cent and starts life in the bottle thin and sharp, which for that matter is atypical for Australian and many other New World wines.

In line with that style, the current school of thought considers light-bodied dry white Girgentina varietal wines to be too pure and forthright to benefit from wood ageing. The few wines around made entirely or in part from Girgentina have not been fermented or matured in barriques.

Then again, by using Malta's prominent white variety Girgentina innovatively to liven up blends, for example, the much fleshier Chardonnay and the even fatter and naturally flabby Viognier or possibly the not so tart Malta grown Sauvignon Blanc, structure and nuance might very well be heightened by a subtle, appropriate touch of oak.

Winemakers might even be tempted to go extreme and try and vinify the spritzig Girgentina into a semi or full sparkling white wine. The idea of blending rare indigenous grapes into cuvées for refined (low-alcohol) spumante is by no means a new one and convincingly practised by Italian neighbours using the Méthode Champagnoise and Cuve Close. It yet remains to be tried.

One thing is for certain, though. It would be a shame not to try and safeguard the Maltese indigenous grape varieties and not just for patriotic or romantic reasons. After all, the current fashion in the worldwide wine trade is a preference for well-made wines from indigenous varieties. This trend is just as likely to be an expression of Chardonnay fatigue and customers' boredom with Cabernet as it is an endorsement of fundamental quality or character preference for less unknown grape varieties.

Simply put, the current international vogue for things indigenous may or may not just be a vote of confidence for something new on the market. But, it is almost as if market forces are set to ensure that a varietal Darwinism will prevail, where the best-tasting and best-selling innovators flourish and consumer preference dictates what endures.

### GIRGENTINA IN MALTA

All bush trained but ongoing experiments with Guyot.

Most widely planted variety of all.

Used in blends and as a single (still and frizzante) varietal by Delicata.

### ĠELLEWŻA IN MALTA

High yielder like Girgentina.

Not as widespread as assumed.

Excellent for rosés and good for stone-crunchy light-bodied reds.

### OTHER NATIVES

Other red and white native grapes might subsist, but not in commercially viable tonnage.

'Catalana' and 'Marsus Tan-Nahla' have been mentioned.

# The New Grapes on the Block

Besides the commercially viable indigenous grape varieties Girgentina and Ġellewża, new grapes are claiming their own on the vineyard block in Malta. But, how do different grape varieties result in wines that are different in taste? How do the interplay of Maltese climate and soil and the skills of local winemakers affect the flavour of Malta grown wines made from the foreign root-settlers? Time to pause and taste, but where does one begin?

The global world of grapes and wine is a rather democratic and open-minded one – a far cry from the world of politics and business where segregation creeps in. Therefore, when reviewing the grape varieties that are relatively new additions to the Maltese vinescape, international white and red grape varieties (noble or not) have not been painstakingly separated either.

If there is need for one, a thin and feeble thread weaves their story together; tying one end of the string to Syrah, Malta's anchor in the world's ocean of wine, the other end tousled up in the sweet promise of Moscato.

From the onset of the planting of international varieties in Malta, Rhône varieties appeared to thrive especially well in a number of Maltese soils. Of all the wines hailed as Malta's greatest ever, the best ones made from Syrah might very well turn out to be potential candidates for the sacrosanct title of 'Super Maltese' – vinified into a blend or as a stand-alone varietal.

The question being begged now is whether the mind's eye of Maltese winemakers will fall on the other planted Rhône varieties that are bearing fruit. Raised under the right conditions in the vineyard and brought up with lots of love and care in the winery, capricious cropper red Carignan and the 'hot' white grape variety Viognier might be as good a base as Grenache Noir for different styles of top-quality Malta grown wines.

The Burgundy born darling Chardonnay and Loire prize-grape Sauvignon Blanc are very different from each other and yet Maltese winemakers succeed in making remarkable wines from these two noble varieties. The Malta grown wines made from either grape variety remain true to the grape's characteristics. Together with Girgentina, Chardonnay as well as Sauvignon Blanc, blended into the most unique and inimitable blends, they could result in highly marketable and, more importantly, enjoyable wines that show 'typicity'.

In today's new-wave Maltese wines, Merlot seems the best vinous canvas for Maltese vintners in search of self-expression and wanting to encapsulate a taste of Malta's own 'terroir'. Wine whisperers say Merlot is tomorrow's promise when grown on not too heavy clay soils and has perhaps more potential than its cousins Cabernet Sauvignon and Franc.

And, last but not least, how about the Muscat family, also known as Moscato, that quintessentially Mediterranean variety that also grows in Malta?

Will anyone try his hand at crushing the grapiest of all grapes and bring about the first sweet Malta grown white wine?

# Syrah – The Global Grape

'Shsss..y…rahgsh', harsh as it sounds in Maltese, is the buzz word in Maltese wine circles. It has been for a while now. But where does it come from, that adoptive grape?

Few people agree about the origin of the grape that is known nowadays as Syrah, a name that crosses one's lips in the same breath as the famous wines of the Rhône Valley in France.

It could have been taken there via several plausible routes from the similarly-titled city of Shiraz in what is now Iran. Others believe the Roman legions of Probus might have brought the vine north from the Egyptian vineland via Syracuse in Sicily and encouraged plantings in Gaul. In fact, there seem to be historical accounts of Cleopatra drinking Syrah wines while bathing in goat's milk (which is better than the other way round).

But recent research and DNA profiling have clearly shown that what is Syrah to the French and Shiraz to the Australians (who have espoused the variety) is indeed indigenous to France. Syrah is actually a genetic cross between two less noble varieties, Mondeuse Blanc and Dureza.

Syrah is often nicknamed 'the global grape' as its popularity is growing rapidly. This is understandable. Syrah is capable of producing superb wines across the spectrum: from simple, easy drinking to the sublime concentration of Hermitage and Cornas and the more perfumed Côte Rôtie in France. Like Cabernet, it has a skin full of dense, dark fruit and tannin. When vinified well, all sorts of dark berry fruits jump out of the glass and wines with barrel-ageing can develop an enchanting tarry, leathery, smoky character.

There are different styles of Syrah seen around the world – whether as the principal grape variety in a blend or as the sole variety in a wine. The most renowned plantings of old Shiraz vines are found in Australia, especially in the Barossa Valley, and it is at home in the Hunter Valley. In the hands of perfectionists, Syrah is distinctive and pioneering winemakers are taking Syrah across myriad climates and soil types. Syrah or Shiraz is conquering new terroirs in South Africa, California, New Zealand, Chile, Spain, Italy and Malta too.

Above all, Syrah is adaptable to most growing conditions and soil types, but the variety prefers sunny, rocky hillsides rather than valley floors. It is happiest with its feet in well-drained, and unforgiving, poor soils. Thus, Malta's land appears to offer a good home for this sun-loving cropper.

The arrival of Syrah in Malta is easy to chart. The Maltese vineyards planted with Syrah are still very young - the oldest having been planted between seven to ten years ago. Maltese bottlings of inexpensive Syrah are few, but mono-varietal, unoaked examples show the typical varietal characteristics best.

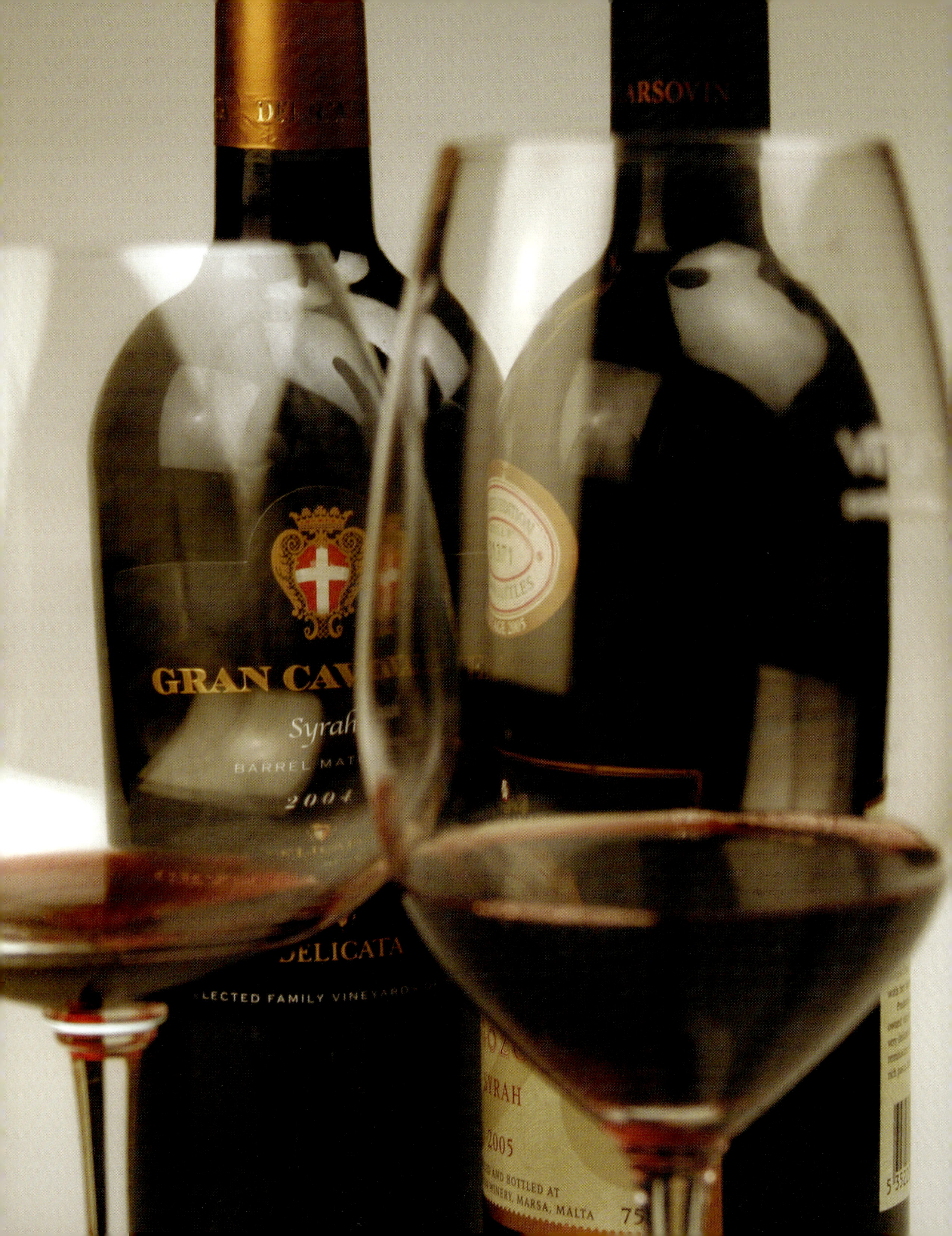
Syrah
2004
SYRAH
2005
BOTTLED AT
WINERY, MARSA, MALTA

Syrah has not yet been vinified into a spicy, sparkling red. There are however examples of dual-acts with Cabernet Sauvignon and a cheerful ménage à trois with Rhône cultivars Carignan and Grenache as well as an atypical concubine of Merlot blended with Ġellewża.

The better (and more expensive) Malta grown, stand-alone varietal bottlings already embody the character of the grape in a way that inspires, marrying fresh acidity with voluptuous texture, delivering a complexity of earth, game, leather and berry as well as slightly herbal aromas.

Surprisingly, premium Maltese Syrah already tastes refined despite the tender age of the vines, whilst the quality of wine produced generally tends to improve as the vines mature. Probably, this is thanks to careful site selection, low yields and a winemaker's respect for concentration of flavour and gentle upbringing in French and American oak.

Malta grown Syrah is concentrated, deep and violet-like in colour. Very distinct is its nose: prickling spices, herbal and rich, black fruit dashed with freshly crushed black pepper. In general, Malta grown Syrah is approachable at a younger age than wines coming from the Northern Rhône. The characteristics are not unlike those of better French examples, usually with an extra layer of ripeness as found in the styles of the Californian self-styled Rhône Rangers, who make their Syrah in the French model too.

Hopefully, Maltese winemakers will do what Syrah trailblazers all over the world tend to do when they believe that their place is the recipient of the Holy Grail – throw caution to the wind and go for broke. There should surely be more Maltese Syrah around to be enjoyed.

**SYRAH IN MALTA**

Syrah is the familiar name in Malta, although Shiraz is permissible too.

As a single varietal first by Meridiana, then Delicata and recently Marsovin and Camilleri Wines.

Delicata produce a unique soft, unoaked mono varietal as well as a powerful Shiraz-Cab blend, emulated by Camilleri Wines.

**SYRAH IN THE VINEYARD**

Likes unforgiving, poor soils, rocky hillsides

Introduced in the Maltese vineyard in the 1990s

Grows vigorously, good disease resistance.

Keeping yields low is crucial for quality in the bottle.

**SYRAH IN THE GLASS**

Deep, violet-like red colour Dark berries, black pepper, cloves, thyme and bay leaves, 'sweaty saddle' or leather.

With bottle age, more flowery and scents of sweet cedar wood and cigar box at best

Ageing potential of Malta grown Syrah will increase as vines mature.

GRAPE AWAKENINGS

# Grenache – and other Rhône Grapes

GRENACHE NOIR is another dark-skinned grape variety that has found favour only recently. In Malta, it is seen on labels together with the harsher Syrah and Carignan as it fills out a sappy, soft and light-bodied, unwooded Maltese red wine.

It is an interesting grape variety, that Grenache Noir, and a typical hot climate vine, too. It is a strong and rigid plant, which can be trained in the bush method or on wired trellises as is the case in the Maltese vineyards. It does well in dry and windy climates, buds early, ripens very well and late.

Logically, Grenache Noir grows as well in Malta as it does in the rest of the Mediterranean basin. Grenache – Garnacha in Spain – is Spanish by heritage, but the Sardinians who still call it Cannonau, would argue that the Spaniards nicked their indigenous grape during the island's four centuries of Spanish occupation.

Grenache is most commonly known for yielding France's popular reds from the Rhône Valley, where it is used on its own or together with other varieties for a simple Côtes-du-Rhône to a more complex Châteauneuf-du-Pape.

But this variety comes into a class of its own as a pink wine. The grape has everything going for it and the one word that encapsulates the Turkish Delight-coloured rosés like Delicata's Medina Vineyards Rosé made solely from Malta grown Grenache Noir is 'respect'.

Excellent colour has been extracted from the grape's light red coloured skins. It is such an ideal ingredient for making rosé wines, which, by the way, are almost made exactly like white wines.

But unlike when making white wine, when producing a rosé wine the grape juice has to be left in contact with the dark-coloured skins for a brief period of time before the fermentation process. Twenty-four hours at cool temperatures (between 12 and 17 degrees Celsius) is about spot on to extract just enough anthocyanins out of the red skins to tint the dull grey grape juice of the Grenache Noir berries bright pink.

For rosés, great care must be taken to preserve the fresh, primary aromas from the moment the ripe grapes are collected to the final stages of the bottling of the finished wine. Hand-picking is a prerequisite. Computerised cooling systems and careful refrigeration have to be applied throughout the entire vinification process; from the moment the fragile berries are crushed (and in particular at the stage of fermentation), or when converting natural sugars into alcohol by adding single strains of cultured, winemaking yeast. This takes place in modern, closed stainless steel tanks at controlled temperatures between 15 and 20 Celsius.

It is a very worthwhile experience to taste Malta grown Grenache rosé side by side with Tavel, made on the right bank of the Rhône, other dry rosés from Lirac,

MEDINA
VINEYARDS
ROSÉ GRENACHE
MALTA GROWN
Vintage
2005
HAND PICKED GRAPES
DELICATA
SELECTED FAMILY VINEYARDS OF MALTA

located just north of Tavel, and a variety of other rosés from Provence further down South, which are all made from this grape variety.

It is guaranteed to leave you in awe for the pristine aromatic nose of the Malteser. When drunk young, Malta grown medium-dry rosé is extremely lively and shows off a lovely raspberry nose, dusted with scents of white pepper and wild thyme. Unlike a host of 'donut' rosés around it has good weight and anything but a hollow middle palate.

CARIGNAN is a different red Rhône cultivar that is relatively new to Malta. Its main characteristic is astringency, which becomes apparent when tasted on its own before disappearing into a blend as it often does in a number of wine producing countries. Camilleri tried to market a cult rosé blend of Carignan and Grenache for what they have dubbed 'the young and furious wine-funsters'.

In southern Sardinia it is rightly hailed in the rich and supple Carignano del Sulcis. Thus far, however, there is no Maltese single varietal wine made from Carignan. It might do extremely well though in warm Malta; especially when exposed to the saline sea breeze (on the small island of Comino perhaps), provided that vignerons keep down the vine's vigour and crop size. This may result in fruity and nicely concentrated red wines with modern appeal.

Thanks to the variety's tolerance to saline ambient conditions, which make life tough for pests in the vineyard, it might well be the most suitable grape variety in Malta for organic farming in the near future.

VIOGNIER, actually a white grape émigré from the Rhône, on the other hand, is a shy fruit bearer and its grapes are somewhat low in acidity. Neither are there any Maltese examples of Viognier around, although the grape variety has been planted in Malta in small numbers.

This is the 'designer' white grape variety responsible for most of the dry white wines produced in the terraced vineyards in and around Condrieu in the northern Rhône. Other very tasty but usually expensive examples come from Australia and California, the grape's new realm.

When vinified with great care and skill, these creamy single varietal wines are voluptuously scented with freesias, orange blossoms, peaches and apricot. Viognier has a reputation for being all too difficult to get right, both in the vineyard and the winery - and it will be fascinating to see what Maltese winemakers can do with it.

### GRENACHE IN MALTA

May be bush trained or wire trellised.

Wonderful as a rosé by Delicata and Marsovin, and in a light-bodied red blend by Delicata.

### CARIGNAN IN MALTA

High yielder.

Good blender at present; maybe tomorrow's new single varietal.

Potential for Malta grown wine made from organically cultivated grapes.

### VIOGNIER IN MALTA

Plantings are few; treacherous but challenging in the vineyards.

Might blend well with Girgentina and Sauvignon Blanc besides Chardonnay.

# Chardonnay – The Submissive Darling

Chardonnay, the name of the globe's most popular white grape, was virtually unheard of 30 years ago when people used to drink Chablis and Chassagne. Today, Chardonnay is the C-buzzword on labels and for most wine drinkers, white wine is simply Chardonnay. It is the ultimate crowd-pleaser and appeals the world over to consumers and winemakers alike.

Chardonnay probably originated in Burgundy, France, as a cross of two varieties, the nearly distinct light-berried Gouais Blanc and the Pinot Noir. Chardonnay is no longer confined to French soil, though. Meanwhile, this globetrotter of a grape has travelled to every wine-producing country, from Chile to China, from England to Peru.

The variety's ability to almost uniformly produce excellent wines has spurred an increase in Chardonnay plantings in Malta and Gozo, too, especially since the late 1990s. Vines grow well in a variety of local soil types and the Maltese benign Mediterranean climate suits Chardonnay just fine. Grapes ripen and are hand-picked near the beginning of August, making it one of the earliest Chardonnay harvests in the Northern Hemisphere.

In the Maltese Islands, Chardonnay is now the most widely planted international white grape variety. As raw material, it is so pliable that it has become the darling grape of winemakers, who love the variety because they can tailor the wine to everyone's aspirations, both theirs and the consumer's. Interestingly, the Chardonnay grape itself does not have a particularly strong flavour or aroma in itself, but is rather neutral.

The advantage is that the wine may turn out to be a 'picture postcard' of where the Chardonnay grapes are grown. Although the finished wine may vary widely based on local grape growing conditions, winemaking techniques can help shape a Chard's profile immensely. With little personality of its own, the Chardonnay grape easily submits to and expresses the will of the winemaker and lets itself be turned into a wider range of wines varying in style and quality than any other grape.

In Malta, too, there is an assortment of still wines made from Chardonnay, either vinified on its own or blended with another grape variety, either fermented or aged in oak barriques or simply left unwooded. It is even turned into a bone-dry sparkling wine in the méthode traditionelle. The wines are nearly always dry and often fairly full-bodied, which can be enjoyed with a wide variety of flavourful dishes including both meat and fish.

Of course, regardless of their origin, all wines made from Chardonnay show common characteristics. It is just that, depending on where the grapes have ripened, a Chardonnay will taste more of apple, pear or lemon - in cooler climates - or perhaps more of pineapple or melon and honey - in warmer areas.

Although the average age of Maltese vines is still young, most Chardonnays about already demonstrate fine varietal qualities. In as far as it exists; typical Malta grown Chardonnay shows good colour and weight. It is fruit-driven, lush and ripe, rather than floral or mineral in character.

Malta grown Chardonnay has a nice level of acidity and the single varietal wines are almost incapable of being tart. A crisper and unique blend, though, is the lively marriage between Maltese Chardonnay and the sharper indigenous, white Girgentina variety, which lifts the unwooded wine's freshness.

Other Maltese premium bottlings of Malta grown Chardonnay entice with flavours of mango, peach and sometimes dried fruits and go to show how well wood and white wine can work together when left in the hands of a skilled winemaker. These barrel fermented or cask matured Chards make a substantial buttery and creamy impact on the palate, often arguably more than on the nose, which may have a pleasant New Worldish twang of citrus to it - not unlike the cooler Californian counterparts. Hints of toasty vanilla and butterscotch add another dimension - and some ageing potential - to some of these medal-winning Maltese Chardonnays.

To get a palate snapshot of 'Maltese Chardonnay', you will need to taste more examples of it than of any other Malta grown grape variety, which is rarely a penitential occupation.

### CHARDONNAY IN MALTA

As easy drinking to full-bodied single varietals by Delicata, Marsovin, Meridiana and novice Camilleri Wines.

As a crisp double-act with Girgentina by Delicata and most recently also by Marsovin.

As a sparkler called Cassar de Malte by Marsovin.

### CHARDONNAY IN THE VINEYARD

Buds early and the harvest is as early as first week August.

Time of harvest is crucial to avoid over-ripeness and flabby wines.

Most widely planted white variety in Malta and Gozo.

### CHARDONNAY IN THE GLASS

Greenish tinge to golden yellow in colour.

Top Chards keep up to 5 years in bottle, but are best when drunk young.

Do not over-chill premiums into submission.

Subtle, no overpowering use of oak.

GRAPE AWAKENINGS

# Pinot Blanc – or Bianco

Like its cousin Chardonnay, Pinot Blanc comes originally from Burgundy. Although this white grape variety can still be found in a few vineyards there, Pinot Blanc or Klevner has now its home in Alsace. In Germany it goes by the name of Weisburgunder.

As in neighbouring Italy, in Malta the variety is also known as Pinot Bianco. It was introduced into the Maltese vineyards in the late 1990s but has not yet captured the imagination of Maltese winemakers. Neither can it be spotted on labels of Malta grown wines, which would probably turn out to be fairly simple but fleshy and crisp dry white examples with an indistinct perfume.

Hardly ever does Pinot Blanc reach the heights of the more flamboyant Chardonnay. Because of its tart profile and high acidity, however, the pale grape makes for good blending material. Pinot Blanc or Bianco goes well together with Chardonnay for the making of dry sparkling wines; especially in warm climate wine producing countries such as Malta.

# Sauvignon Blanc – Sincerely Fussy

Sauvignon Blanc is a white grape variety that produces the type of wines you either love or hate. Typical Sauvignon Blanc has very distinct and recognisable characteristics and particularly great appeal for those who appreciate crisp, dry white wines with a piercing, assertive aroma.

This is a very fashionable grape and Sauvignon Blanc also has its roots firmly entrenched in French soil. Some of France's most highly regarded wines are made from this noble variety and for a long time, the upper Loire and the twin appellations Sancerre and Pouilly Fumé in particular, provided the flinty, edgy benchmark style in which grassy, nettle and mineral flavours are more prominent.

Undoubtedly, Sauvignon Blanc thrives best in a cool climate and for long it was kept out of the vineyards in the New World. But since the 1980s winemakers in Marlborough at the north of New Zealand's South Island have blazed the trail by making examples that combine a particular mouth-watering clarity with a touch of crunchy gooseberry fruit. Other countries that have become renowned for their Sauvignon Blanc are Chile, Australia, South Africa and Italy. In California Robert Mondavi started a Sauvignon league of his own by making an oak-aged version re-christened as Fumé Blanc.

In Malta, winemaker Emmanuel Delicata produces the island's only noted Sauvignon Blanc, although Camilleri winery has access to a substantial tonnage of Sauvignon Blanc grapes too. It is unwooded, of course, lower in acidity and misses the 'attack' of the renowned French wines but compares fairly well with other pungently catty examples coming from the Languedoc or other bordering Mediterranean and Central European wine producing countries.

It is nevertheless an elegant, aromatic dry white wine with a Sauvignon Blanc hallmark to it, thanks to the use of a technique called 'macération pelliculaire', which indicates that the fermenting grape juice has remained in contact with the skins to extract maximum flavour. This example sits in the wine rack together with the fuller, more firm and grapey style of Sauvignon Blanc with riper kiwi fruit and slightly more alcohol.

As the young vines get accustomed to the Maltese conditions, Malta grown Sauvignon Blanc will find a good number of fans as it will become more bracing and vibrant with each new vintage. The use of viticultural practices, such as careful pruning and moderate thinning of shoots as to shade the fruit and the early picking of slightly under-ripe grapes, might be instrumental, too, in capturing more 'greenness' in the glass.

In any case, Delicata has forged a path for Maltese Sauvignon Blanc, a crisp wine that goes well with Maltese foods where acidity needs matching – tomato dishes, lemon garnished fish dishes, goat's cheese – and equally, with difficult oily fish where the wine's acidity can act as a foil to richness – think of the local lampuka.

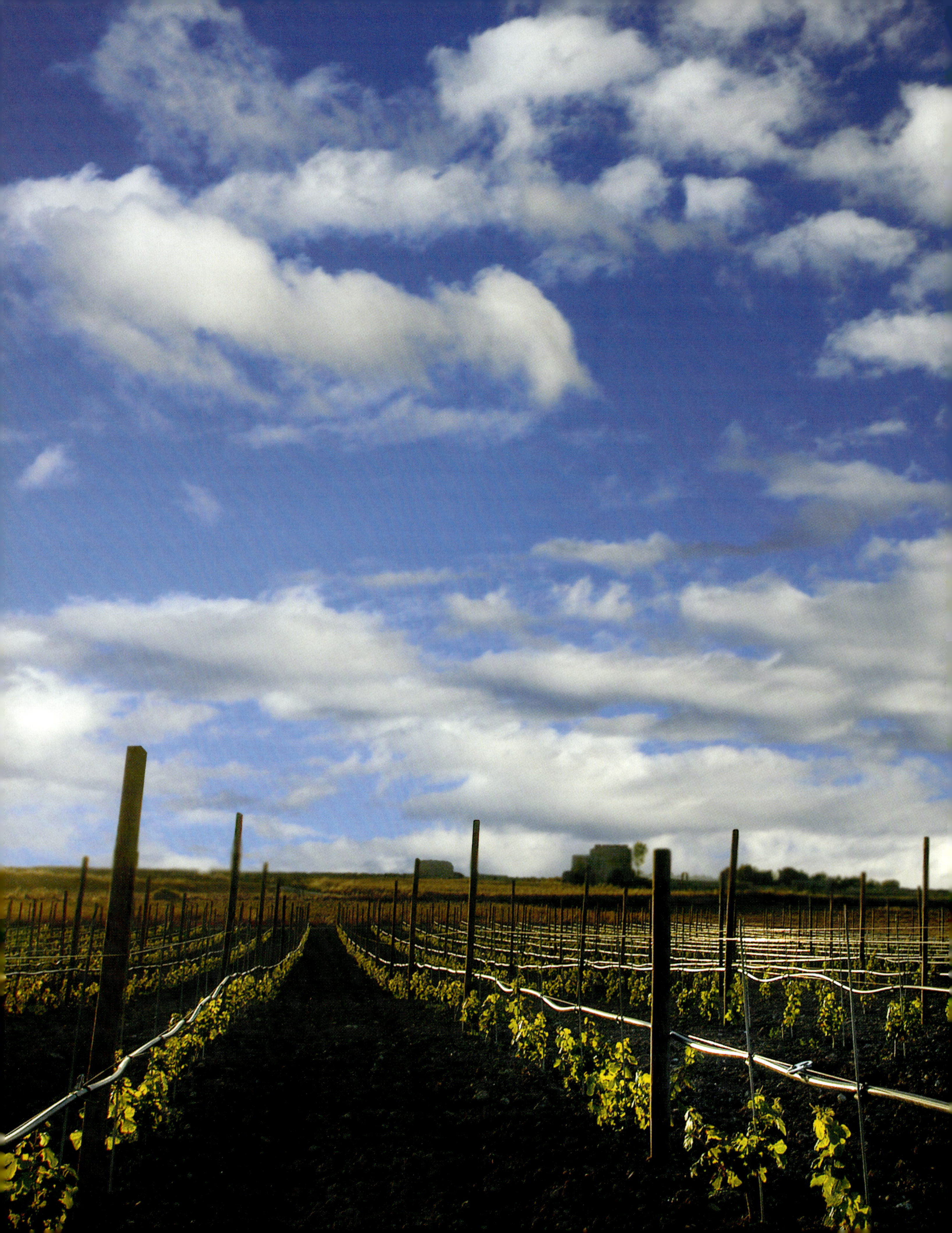

### SAUVIGNON IN MALTA

Commercially only available as one single varietal by Delicata.

Might blend well with ripe Maltese Chardonnay or tarter Girgentina.

### SAUVIGNON IN THE VINEYARD

Possibly irregular production levels in Maltese humid climate.

Leaf canopy management may help produce 'green' or 'grassy' wines.

Excess sunshine results in riper fruit flavours.

### SAUVIGNON IN THE GLASS

Greenish, silver tinge, distinct aroma.

Best drunk as fresh as possible.

Serve well-chilled as an aperitif or with difficult to pair dishes.

# Merlot – The Fruitcake Grape

Malta, and its smaller island of Gozo in particular, are a good-value source of the noble variety Merlot, amicably dubbed Ribena for grown-ups. It is amazing how well Merlot has taken to the Maltese soil in such a short period. The first vintages of Malta grown Merlot already surprise pleasantly with a very velvety texture, flavours reminiscent of blackcurrant and all the plum-like allure of a rich fruitcake.

What's more, when tasting across Malta's red wines made up entirely of Merlot, the desirable 'spice cupboard' aromas dash out the glass. Even when Merlot has been added to relatives Cabernet Sauvignon and Franc, the 'typicity' of Maltese Merlot seems to capture the taster's attention first. There is nearly always a subtle chocolately and dusty, slightly salted attraction to it, regardless of a wine's pedigree.

Historically Merlot blended with Cabernet has always had a supporting role in the wines from the Médoc, a famous Bordeaux appellation south of the river Gironde. Further north on the cooler and damp 'right bank', Merlot plays the main part, and stars almost solo in the wines of the St-Emilion and Pomerol appellations. Here, the finest of the world's Merlots, such as Château Pétrus and Le Pin, possess great depth, complexity and longevity.

Merlot generally gives wines of a style not too dissimilar to the more austere Cabernet Sauvignon. It is rounder and smoother and Merlot is therefore often used as an elegant and mellowing component to soften the solid structure of Cabernet.

An increasing number of wineries now produce single varietal Merlots in many countries, California and Washington State performing especially well. Elsewhere in the New World, Merlot is gaining field in South Africa and Eurasia. Off the shores of Malta, Merlot as well as Cabernet Franc, has been a favourite in the north of Italy and there are some seriously ambitious examples in Sicily and Greece, too.

Earlier than Cabernet Sauvignon to mature in the bottle, Merlot is held in higher esteem by wine drinkers than by wine collectors whilst winemakers somehow regard Merlot as an understudy of Cabernet Sauvignon. On the Maltese scene, Syrah is spurred on as the country's most promising red variety to render mind-blowing wines in the future but the noble grape Merlot could very well become the next best thing.

The wines so far are encouraging to say the least as they all let true Merlot colours and 'Maltese-ness' shine through at the same time – regardless of the wines' ancestry. Apparently Malta's rocky and arid terrain and even the local clayish soils is a good base for Merlot. The people in the vineyards seem to have a knack of picking grapes that are neither under nor over ripe, which would have made the resulting wines more likely to lean away from their delicious fruity flavours and lush mouthfeel.

### MERLOT IN MALTA

As Bordeaux blends by Marsovin, Camilleri Wines, Meridiana and Delicata.

The latter three producers both make single varietals too.

All brought up in oak except for one by Delicata.

### MERLOT IN THE VINEYARD

Loves the rocky, arid terrain and suited to clay soils in particular.

Cabernet Sauvignon without the growing pains.

Moderate to high yields and potential top quality.

### MERLOT IN THE GLASS

Best drunk after one to three years of bottle age.

Some unfiltered bottlings may throw lots of sediment.

One vintner's use of oak is not another's.

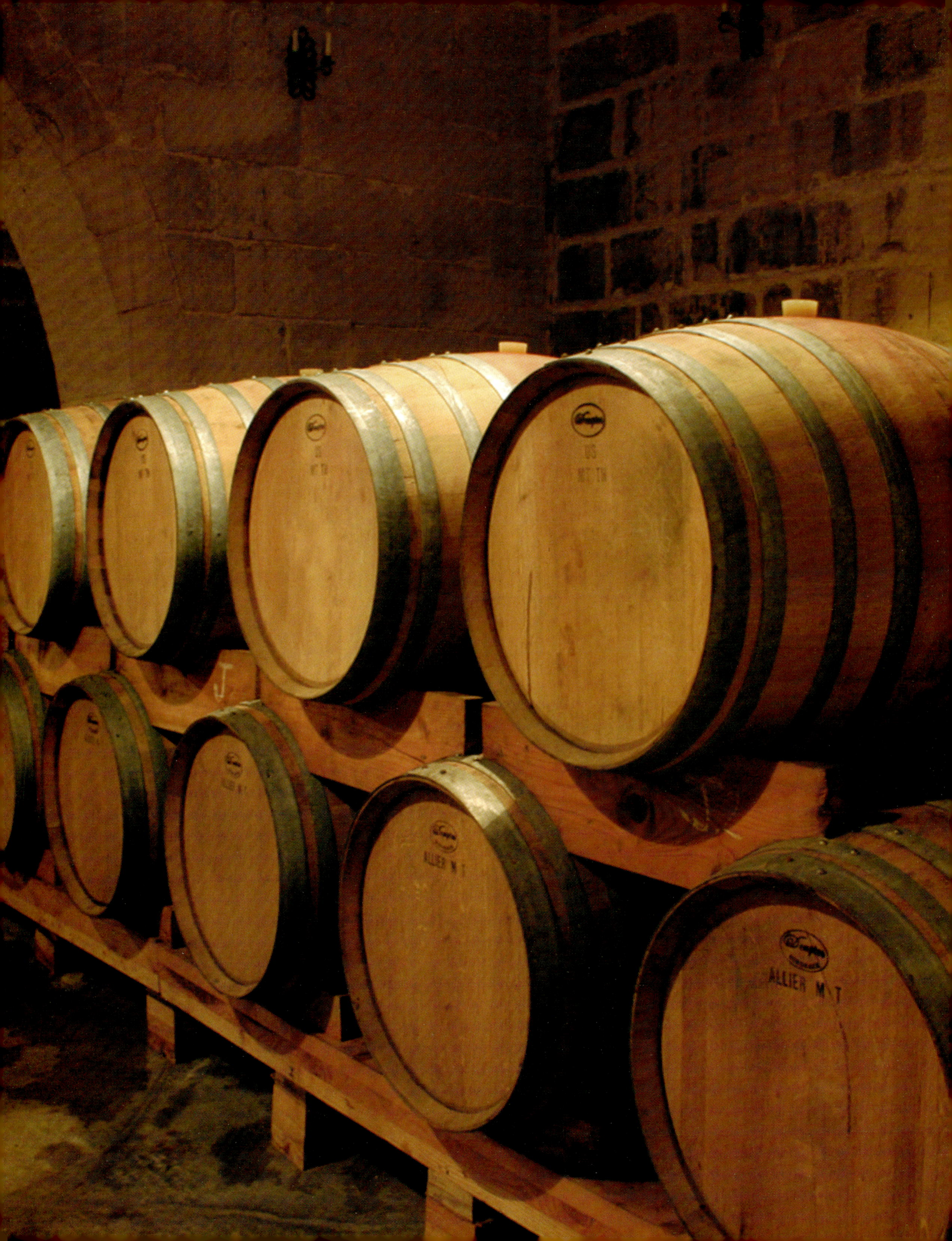
ALLIER

# Cabernet Sauvignon – and Franc

Famous, fabulous and fabled, Cabernet Sauvignon hardly needs an introduction. Its reputation precedes this adaptable red grape variety that through different regional styles (varying from cigar box-like to eucalyptus overlaid) remains true to itself wherever it sets its roots.

Cabernet Sauvignon's heartland is Bordeaux. Here the rather tannic wines are suited to maturing in oak casks and are never jammy but mineral in style. Sublime are the greatest growths of the area, the crus classés, which provide sensual as well as intellectual stimulation.

But Cabernet is no longer only the preserve of France. Since the 1960s, Cabernet has been on a long journey around the globe, travelling from the Old to the New World. Its attraction is now rapidly nudging southward through Italy into Sicily and around the whole of the Mediterranean including Malta, too.

The complete list of the best wine producing regions for Cabernet Sauvignon is lengthy. This black grape variety is very adaptable to a number of soils and climates. It appears throughout Central Europe, South America, USA, New Zealand, Australia and South Africa.

Depending on the country where the thick-skinned grapes are ripened, the respective Cabernets are medium- to full-bodied. Generally, the wines are distinguished by their intense aroma as well as their blackcurrant flavour and good length. The balance between good acidity and a high level of tannin makes Cabernet-based wines ideal candidates for cellaring, which pays off dividends in the form of a complex bouquet.

Although Cabernet Sauvignon tends to run with all the glory, often it is found in a blend together with softer, juicier varieties such as Merlot and the most common 'other grape' Cabernet Franc.

In fact, the lesser tannic Cabernet Franc is, together with Sauvignon Blanc the genetic parent of the more cosmopolitan Cabernet Sauvignon. It can be found in Washington and from New York to New Zealand, but most Cabernet Franc is picked in France where it is planted mainly for blending purposes. Cabernet Franc also grows in abundance in Romania, Hungary, the Balkans, the Friuli region of northeastern Italy and in Malta as well.

Supporters Marsovin put it to use in almost every red wine blend of theirs and vinify this rather vegetative red grape together with a touch of Syrah into a good toothsome red, which is lighter in body and more herbaceous in comparison to a Maltese wine made only from Cabernet Sauvignon.

Most of the Maltese premium red wines that rely heavily on Cabernet Sauvignon, though, are a méritage, a term coined to refer to the universal type of red wines made by blending Cabernet Sauvignon with the aforementioned classic Bordeaux varieties Merlot, Cabernet Franc, and maybe some Petit Verdot as well. A pinch of Petit Verdot, another

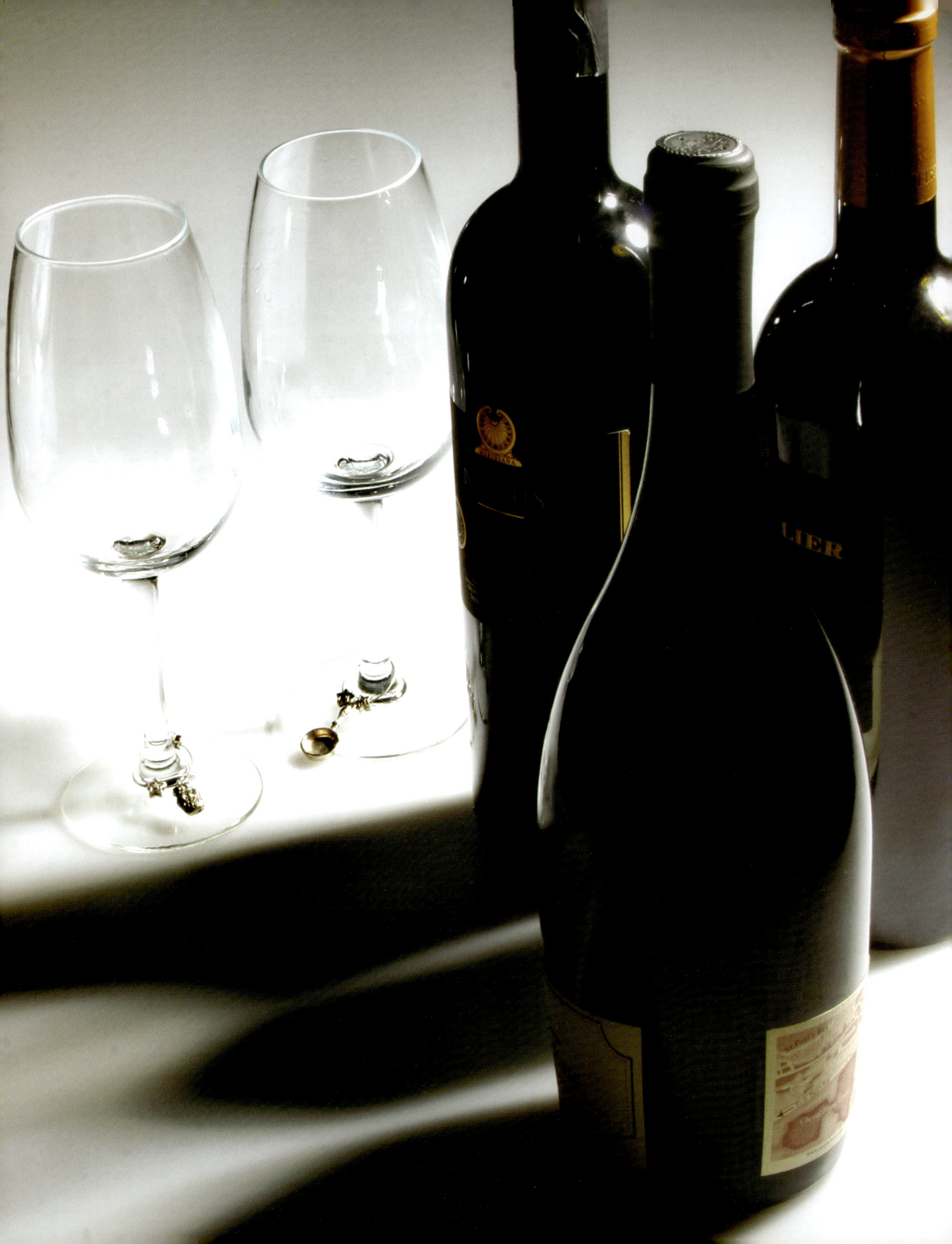

red Bordeaux variety that has also found footing in the Maltese Islands, is usually added to spice up the finished wine.

In some instances, Maltese winemakers consciously and skilfully add more or less equal parts of Merlot to Cabernet Sauvignon to produce quality red duo-blends. In blind tastings, it is not unusual to mistake the better full-bodied vinous tandems for elegant Sonoma Cabernet from USA's Golden State, which has it from fruit more than whopping power, for instance. In other words, these Malta grown reds are rather classic in style than the syrupy, loose-knit type and perhaps the key to success here is indeed a judicious upbringing in French and American oak barriques.

Unoaked straight Maltese Cabernet, on the other hand, tastes somewhat different and is pleasantly upfront, clean, sappy and well balanced, impressing the palate with cassis flavours. When the wine has not been softened by leaving it to mature in oak casks, it has a nice stone crunchiness to it.

On the palate unwooded Cabernet could feel a bit angular, but it will make up for it with definite varietal character. Understandably, stand-alone varietal Malta grown Cabernet Sauvignon might still lack some backbone since the vines still need to come of age. Then again, judging by the early results, Cabernet as a single varietal Maltese wine may eventually very well make its mark. The latest additions to the range of enjoyable reds are blends, though - a practice inspired by Down Under. Cabernet Sauvignon is since recently also being teamed up with its traditional Australian blending partner Shiraz. The combination of Maltese Cabernet Sauvignon and Shiraz grown under the hot Maltese sun does work. The spicier and fleshier Shiraz or Syrah fills out the middle palate and the oak-aged finished wine is worthy of note - and sampling - because of its depth.

In general, none of these wines fall into the trap of too high alcohol, and at around 12 per cent they are the kind of red wines that you finish without trouble. Malta grown Cabernet is a speciality value source for fruit balanced, but fully flavoured wines of thoroughly exportable taste.

So far, Cabernet Sauvignon has not yet been blended with Tempranillo, although this grape variety too is grown in Malta and has already been turned into mono-varietals – sometimes with a typical recognisable scent and flavour of strawberry. Tempranillo is Spanish in origin and goes well with Cabernet. This quality variety takes its name from temprano which implies that it ripens early - unlike Sangiovese, the grape of Chianti, Brunello di Montalcino and Vino Nobile di Montepulciano in Italy. Late ripener Sangiovese, which is also available to Maltese winemakers, however, still awaits vinification in Malta either on its own or also in blends together with Cabernet Sauvignon perhaps.

### CABERNET IN MALTA

As Bordeaux blends by Delicata, Marsovin, Meridiana and Camilleri.

Delicata and recently Camilleri produce also a straight Cabernet Sauvignon and a (Gozo grown) Shiraz-Cab blend.

Marsovin make a Cabernet Franc red with a touch of Syrah but discontinued their all Cab rosé.

### CABERNET IN THE VINEYARD

Cabernet Sauvignon is widely planted and prefers well drained, white soils.

Parent Cabernet Franc is not so common.

There's also some acreage planted with Dr. H.P. Olmo's crossing Ruby Cabernet

### CABERNET IN THE GLASS

Oak-aged wines benefit from one to five years bottle ageing.

Some unfiltered bottlings may throw lots of sediment.

A good nose will smell of pencil shavings and a hint of mint overlaying blackcurrant aromas.

GRAPE AWAKENINGS

# The Muscat Family

Muscat is – apart from a Maltese surname – the family name for a number of vine varieties of which Muscat Blanc à Petits Grains is the finest and the most ancient sort. Although Muscat is classified as a white grape variety, the colour of the grape berries varies from greenish yellow through pink to dark brown. Some family members are raised as both wine and table grapes.

Whereas most other wines made from other grape varieties, noble or otherwise, taste quite different to grapes, even the ones they are made from, a wine produced from Muscat almost always tastes extremely grapey.

Muscat is versatile and can be vinified into low alcohol, sweet fizzy white wines or into stronger dry white wines. It is a particularly good raw material for rather alcoholic still sweet wines such as Beaume-de-Venise and other vins doux naturels of France.

Although it grows in most hot climate wine producing regions, Muscat is quintessentially Mediterranean and has strolled from Greece via Italy to the south of France over many centuries. Closer to Tunisia and Malta than to Italy, the Italian off island Pantelleria is the most famous for its Moscatos.

The variety has been planted in Malta as well and is in vigneron circles usually addressed as Moscato (as is customarily in northwest Italy's spumante industry). However, the first generation of sweet Malta grown Moscato wines still needs to be conceived - something lovers of dessert wines definitely will be looking forward to!

# In A Glass Of Their Own

A symbol of national pride, a valuable addition to any meal or drunk simply on its own – wine deserves full care and attention and therefore the most suitable glass possible.

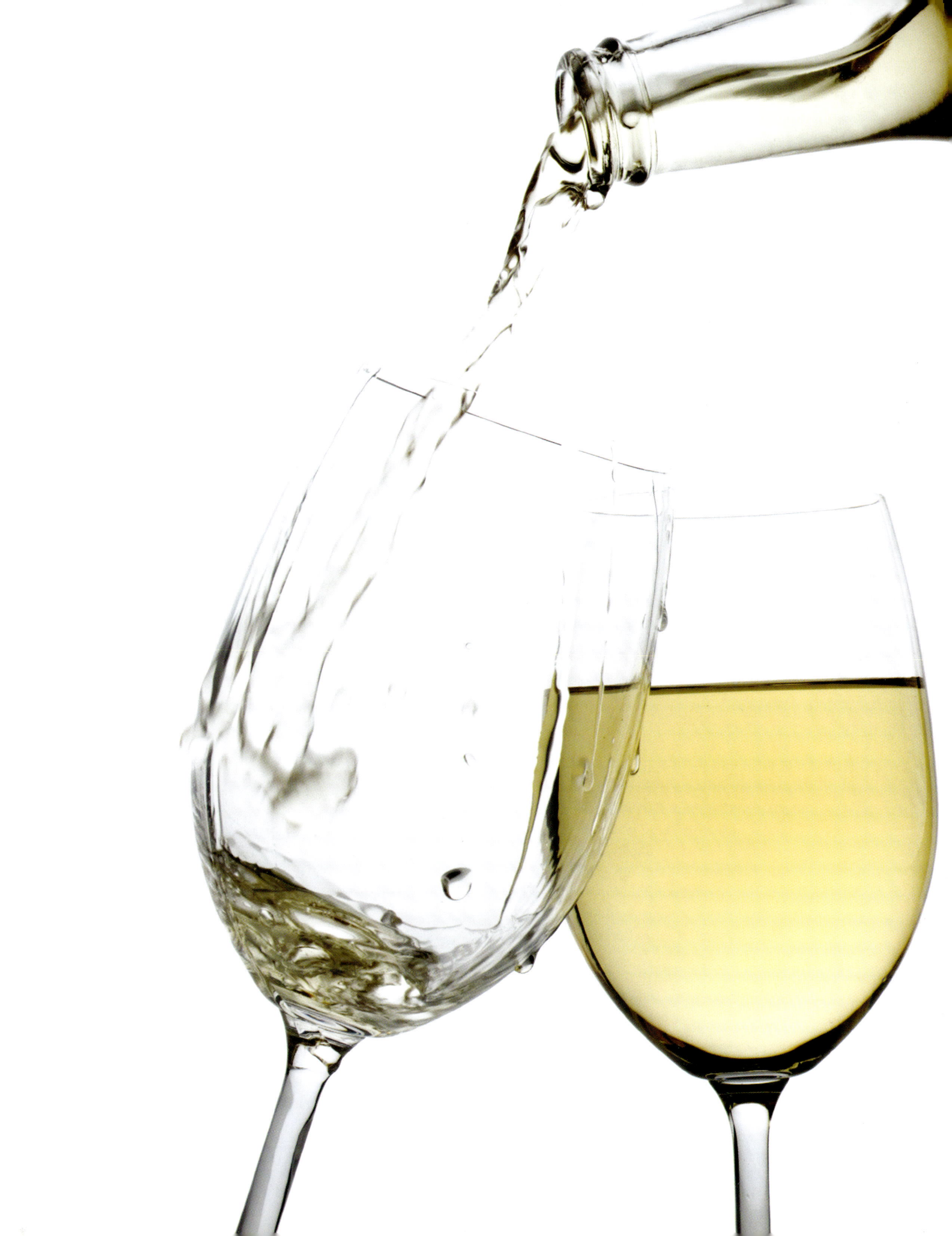

# Clear Cut

The ideal glass for tasting wine is not always the ideal glass for drinking it. But in both cases it is recommended to use a bowl on a stem. This will allow room for twirling and for you to smell the vapours and aromas of the wine that are being pushed upward towards the nose.

A tasting glass should be tulip shaped to channel the aromas and bouquets of finer wines. For drinking purposes one might desire a slightly wider and more comfortable glass that should ideally still be tapered. Preferably all stemware is made of fine crystal-clear glass with a fine rim allowing the taster to commune as physically closely as possible.

There are many fine branded wine glasses around. Various brands of top-quality stemware such as Riedel and Schott Zwiesel offer an array of slightly different glass shapes that have been designed along the principle that how the liquid hits the tongue will affect the taste.

As a rough-and-ready guide for the use of the appropriate shape of stemware, a number of Malta grown wine and glass matches have been test-tasted. The review of the matching game illustrates what type of glass is ideal to use when one really wants to capture the uniqueness and 'typicity' of the different types of wines made from different grape varieties harvested in Malta or Gozo.

Obviously, a specific shape accommodates more than just the one particular wine that has been chosen. Ideally, you endeavour a good number (if not all) of the wines that are similar in make-up and style (as laid out at the end of this section in the wine grids). Duplicating the experiment will prove to be an enjoyable experience for any wine lover. At the risk of stating the obvious, glasses should always be squeaky clean. When dining out in a restaurant get in the habit of smelling the glass before the wine is poured. That way you will not mix up off-smells already in the glass with the scent of the wine.

Apart from spotless and efficient glasses, and choosing the right wine for the occasion, serving each wine at the appropriate temperature also plays a part in its enjoyment. Admittedly, charts which give a degree by degree, wine by wine list of serving temperatures running to dozens of wines can make the prospect of opening any bottle seem like treading a minefield.

However, recommending that white wine be served 'chilled' and red wine at 'room temperature' is pretty vague. The latter old-fashioned diktat is definitely not to be taken literally and over-chilling whites and rosés into aroma-less submission is not wise either. Hopefully, the guide to the most satisfactory temperature for serving each class of Malta grown wines will be helpful.

If anything, in hot Malta, it is advisable to serve whites, rosés and even reds slightly cooler than one normally would. The warm ambient temperature usually quickly nudges up the serving temperature anyhow. And, if you suspect your guests think you've got your reds too cold, you can always impress by saying that you adhere to the cooler, French way of serving.

## TEMPÉRATURES DE SERVICE DES VINS

| | |
|---|---|
| • Vins rouges de grande origine, à maturité Type «BORDEAUX» | 16-17°C. |
| • Vins rouges de qualité ou de grande origine Type «BOURGOGNE» | 15-16°C. |
| • Vins rouges de grande origine encore jeunes | 14-16°C. |
| • Vins rouges légers, fruités et jeunes | 11-12°C. |
| • Vins rosés très fruités nouveaux, primeurs | 10-12°C. |
| • Vins blancs secs de grande origine | 10-12°C. |
| • Petits blancs secs et jeunes | 14-16°C. |
| • «CHAMPAGNE», vins de pays blancs | 10-12°C. |
| • Vins liquoreux et aromatiques mousseux | 8-10°C. |
| | 7-8°C. |
| | 5-6°C. |

# Glass One:
# A Crisp, Dry Girgentina

A dry, white wine made from the indigenous Girgentina is expected to weave a vibrant cascade of green apple and grapefruit flavours right through a bright, zingy finish.

Therefore glasses similar in shape to a 'Loire' bowl should make for a perfect glass-to-wine match. Its distinct long stem tends to slow down any taster's eagerness to indulge and somehow calls for a pause as to reflect on the subtleties of Girgentina.

The medium-sized bowl, with a tapered and slightly tulip shaped aperture, helps to kick off scents of flint - and sweet pea even - without compromising the faint grapey characteristics and warm climate 'typicity' of such a inimitable Maltese white varietal wine.

In fact, the glass's shape and its overall feel enhances the wine's harmonious lightweight texture on the entire palate by dispersing the liquid slightly to the front, but more so towards the middle and the back of the tongue. As a result, it does justice to this aromatic palate teaser.

All in all, this particular glass steers the wine somewhat clear from the sides of one's palate, which are very alert to acidity, yet without masking any of the wine's refreshing shirt-collar-grabbing verve.

# Glass Two:
# Ġellewża Frizzante Rosé

If there is really one style of wine that truly begs for a particular style of glass, it must be Champagne and other full and semi-sparkling wines. Ideally, all these bubbly wines should be served in a 'Champagne flute', which releases the fizziness of the wine more slowly than the saucer-shaped coupe.

Logically, especially semi-sparkling wines such as the locally produced Frizzantes (with fewer bubbles to race to the top) will taste more enjoyable from a narrow and high glass.

It is really pleasurable to sample a semi-sparkling blush or Frizzante rosé made entirely from the unique, indigenous red grape Ġellewża. The flute's crystal thinness allows you to get as close as possible with such an original, stand-alone varietal sparkler. The glass's shape helps show off the distinct fruit-gulpable character of what definitely classifies as an easy-drinking rosé.

Bundles of up-front, silky fruity flavours are balanced by the nice acidity of such a young and fresh deep pink, medium-dry Maltese example. It's easy to get fond of the wine's familiar strawberry-like taste. Amazingly, the appropriate Champagne flute also brings out tinges of perfumed raspberry and the malty richness of what is a very individual and inimitable semi-sparkling wine.

IN A GLASS OF THEIR OWN

# Glass Three:
## Maltese Grenache Noir - Rosé

Today, continents, regions and islands as small as Malta are producing fine wines of unprecedented, new character. Hence, the need for contemporary and functional designed stemware that accommodates these modern and often 'scent and fruit turboed' wines such as, for example, a Maltese rosé wine made entirely form hand-picked Grenache Noir grapes.

Such examples of new-wave, aromatic rosés is best sampled from a glass similar in shape to the so-called 'Alsace' glass rather than from a shorter stemmed and less voluminous, restraining bowl that is customarily used for most French rosé wines such as Tavel from the Rhône Valley and Côtes de Provence, which at times can be slightly hollow.

Malta grown Grenache rosé, however, takes on a lovely Turkish Delight style of pink and is delightfully scented, vibrant, and crammed-packed with strawberry aromas that simply leap out off the glass. The Alsace glass's good height does indeed allow the clean wine's subtle but palpable complexity to be picked up on the nose.

Thanks to the bowl's slightly tulip-shaped contour - as opposed to an aperture with a rim that flares out - this type of glass not only accentuates the rose-petal bouquet and flagrance but also directs the slightly medium-dry wine away from the tip of the tongue towards the back of the palate as to make the very faint tannins detectable whilst leaving plenty refreshing acidity.

IN A GLASS OF THEIR OWN

# Glass Four:
# Light-bodied Malta Grown Red Blends

The custom of chilling certain red wines still raises an eyebrow or two. However, it is indeed good practice to serve light-bodied reds that are low in tannin at a cooler temperature than chambré. Simply taste the freshest vintage of a Syrah, Grenache and Carignan blend. Such a soft and supple red bursts with lively fruit and instant appeal when drunk young. Be adventurous and savour this type of dry red wine, which combines the vivid fruity charm of a white wine with refreshing pleasure when drunken chilled, from a 'Rheingau' glass.

Cinnamon and spice delightfully prickle on the nose, but, admittedly, the low serving temperature does temper the wine's black peppery aromas somewhat. Then again, because this warm-climate red wine is higher in alcohol (11,5 % volume) than most of the aromatic, dry German white wines customarily served from this bowl, the attractive scents of sappy summer fruits are being pushed upward and the blend's vivacity keeps on shining through.

A tulip shaped glass would inappropriately have shot this red wine like an arrow towards the back of the palate where one picks up the bitterness of tannins. The rim of this particular glass, however, flares out and retracts the liquid towards the tip of the tongue, an area that is more alert to sweetness. This is precisely the key to serving an easy-drinking red wine chilled: the proper glass will seem to keep on brimming over with young fruit and mask the tannins so as not to fatigue the palate.

IN A GLASS OF THEIR OWN

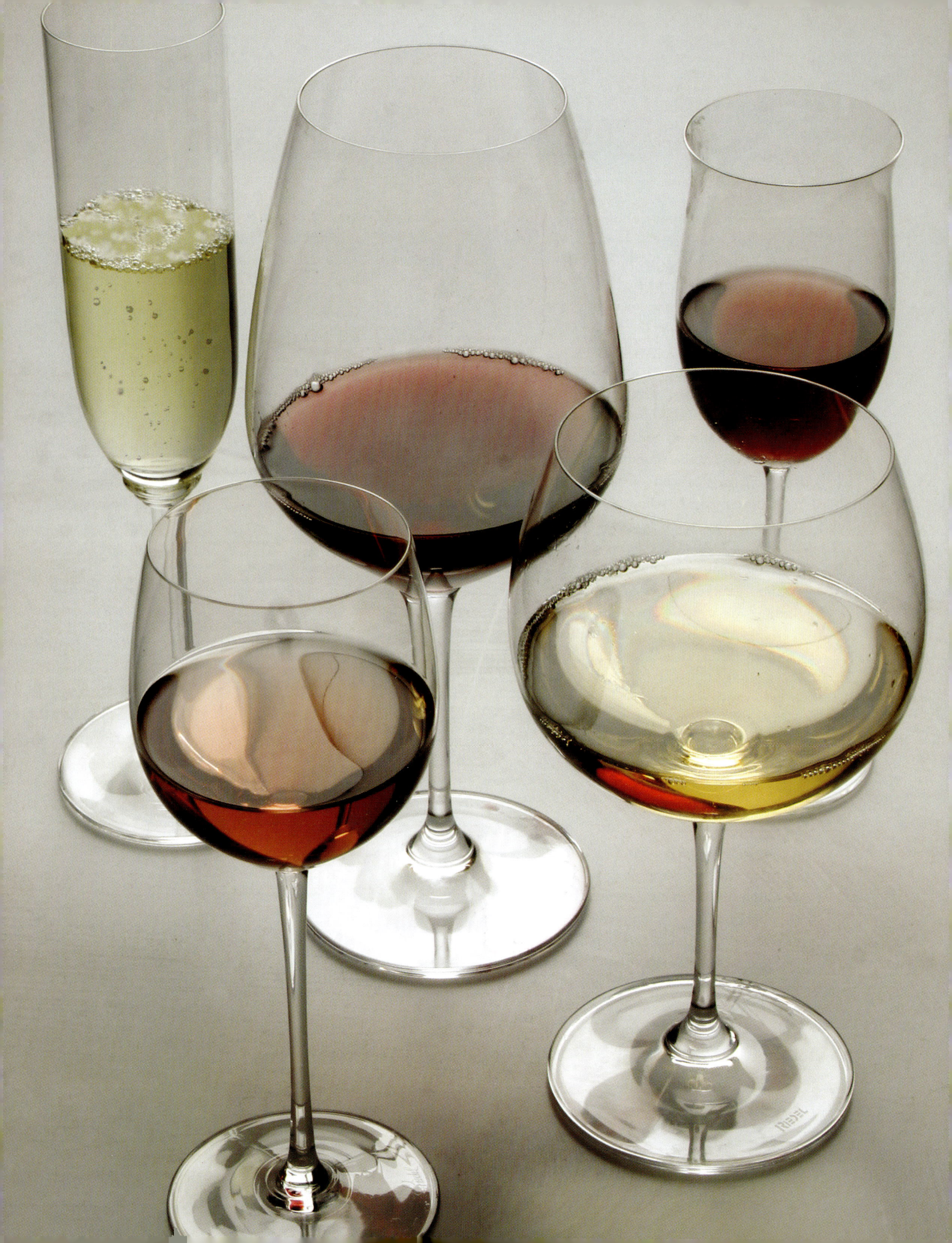
RIEDEL

# Glass Five:
## Premium Maltese Chardonnay Barrel Fermented

Etiquette used to prescribe a smaller glass for white wines than for reds. But why compromise on the size of the bowl if a particular white wine would taste better from a bigger glass? Simply pour less and refill more frequently to keep the white wine in the glass chilled.

There is definitely little pleasure in having to taste a full-flavoured, rich and fat Chardonnay from a constraining glass that fits even a sprightly, bone dry Muscadet as tight as a corset.

Fuller-bodied examples of this noble grape variety in particular need a more abiding 'Montrachet-worthy' glass, which is usually used for Burgundy's finest examples of this variety. Malta grown barrel fermented and/or cask-aged Chardonnay really comes out of the starting blocks. Its bouquet unquestionably delights, but even more so does the glass help in broadening the wine's already complex range of flavours.

Indeed, its bright onset opens up in core fruity flavours reminiscent of citrus-laced pineapple and nectarine; hints of honey-suckle too, turning subtle, rich and long with light toasty, vanilla scented oak in the background, giving a creamy texture and leaving a persistent peanut-butter aftertaste. All in all, the glass's shape accentuates the wine's great balance of power and elegance.

# Glass Six:
# Merlot from Gozo – Barrel Matured

There are still too few examples of full bodied Merlot varietals around made from grapes coming from Gozo. When still young in bottle, Gozo grown Merlot should be decanted prior to pouring it in the glass. Then again, you get away with it when sipping it from an extreme glass with an incredible large inner surface and diameter. This gives the wine extravagant exposure to oxygen and thus a fair chance to 'breathe' in the bowl itself.

'Nosing' the wine is easy and the glass's shape really assists in conveying the message of this oak-aged and youthful but already seductive dry, red wine. Actually, the enjoyment begins with just holding this majestic gourmet glass in your hand, but as soon as you take a sniff, the provenance of the wine as well as the wine's grape variety become very recognisable. The height of the glass allows you to smell through the different layers of aromas and its egg-shape emphasises the wine's fruity and warm climate characteristics.

This fruitcake-like Merlot shows captivating aromas of toffee, a tiny trace of peppermint and, finally, a whiff of new oak too. All the scents are being pushed upward by integrated vapours of alcohol (13% Vol.). The glass delivers the wine mainly to the middle palate.

As expected, a core of blackberry fruit is followed by soft, plummy flavours that turn velvety in texture as the wine fleshes out nicely and lingers on.

# Glass Seven:
# Premium Malta Grown Syrah – Barrel Matured

Malta grown premium Maltese Syrah can be delicious. As a matter of fact, out of all varieties grown in Malta it may be proclaimed as 'the most promising grape'.

A knightly Syrah example of the better vintages compares favourably with elegant European Syrah examples and, possibly, even more so with better Coonawarra Shiraz (rather than with headstrong 'Hunter Hermitage' of the Crocodile Dundee type).

It surely tastes as Syrah is supposed to taste when enjoyed from a massive Gucci type of glass. The royal length of the glass bowl definitely allows the wine's aromatic complexity and intensity to really roar upwards.

The appropriate shape somewhat tames the proud and wilful personality of the latest vintages of what is best described as expressive hot-climate Syrah with a pleasant tang of 'sweaty saddle'. In fact, the glass directs a full-bodied Malta grown red blockbuster right to the middle of the taster's palate.

This pleasantly balances soft mouth-coating tannins and a touch of French oak with the pronounced ripe black fruity characteristics in favour of the wine's delicate gamey and chocolaty flavours.

IN A GLASS OF THEIR OWN

# Basic Tasting Cues

Novices can do with a little practise. Here are a few practical tips on how to get started 'thinking about drinking' in the comfort of one's own home.
It is particularly hard work for the thirsty.

### See clearly
Hold the glass against a plain white background such as a white sheet of paper or cuffs. Hold your hand away from the glass down the stem so as not to obstruct the lighting. Look at the wine from directly above the glass, then at an angle. Do colour, hue and intensity change form the centre towards the rim?

### Swirl and twirl
Aerating the liquid in the glass is the aim. This will releases the volatile aromas. Rehearse swirling with water to minimise stains on your Persian.
Try first to move the glass in small circles on a tabletop. Then hold the stem of a tall tulip shaped glass and handle it like a spoon when stirring a teacup. Now swirl in mid-air…

### Sniff that whiff
Smelling is more important than tasting. Some take a deep whiff. Others smell with one nostril at a time. However, you better hover several times over the wine - just like sniffing a suspicious carton of milk. Pause in between short sniffs so as to avoid fatigue. Closing your eyes may help you concentrate.

IN A GLASS OF THEIR OWN

### Sip and slurp

It sounds funny, but you do it right when your mouth looks like a cat's bottom and you gurgle like a child trying to suck that last drop out of a coke bottle through a straw. Practise slurping mouthwash while you watch yourself in the bathroom mirror. Manoeuvre the wine around your palate.

### Savour or spit

Spitting is the only way to work your way through a lengthy flight of wines and remain standing. Purse your lips and press the wine out in a jet aiming for the receptacle. Keep the spittoon at a safe distance though or it will spit back at you. Keep a napkin handy for that rare dribble.

### Sum it up

Clock your spontaneous impressions of the wine's smell, then the actual taste in your mouth and how the wine's flavour lingers after you have spat it out (or swallowed). Make up your own mind about the wine's intrinsic quality and write this down. Only then check how different the back label reads. Would you buy this bottle again?

# Nipped in the Bud between Madeira and La Mancha

Although many Maltese wines have been bestowed with Gold, Silver and Bronze medals, winning worldwide consumer confidence is all about delivering the message. Quality remains the most universal language.

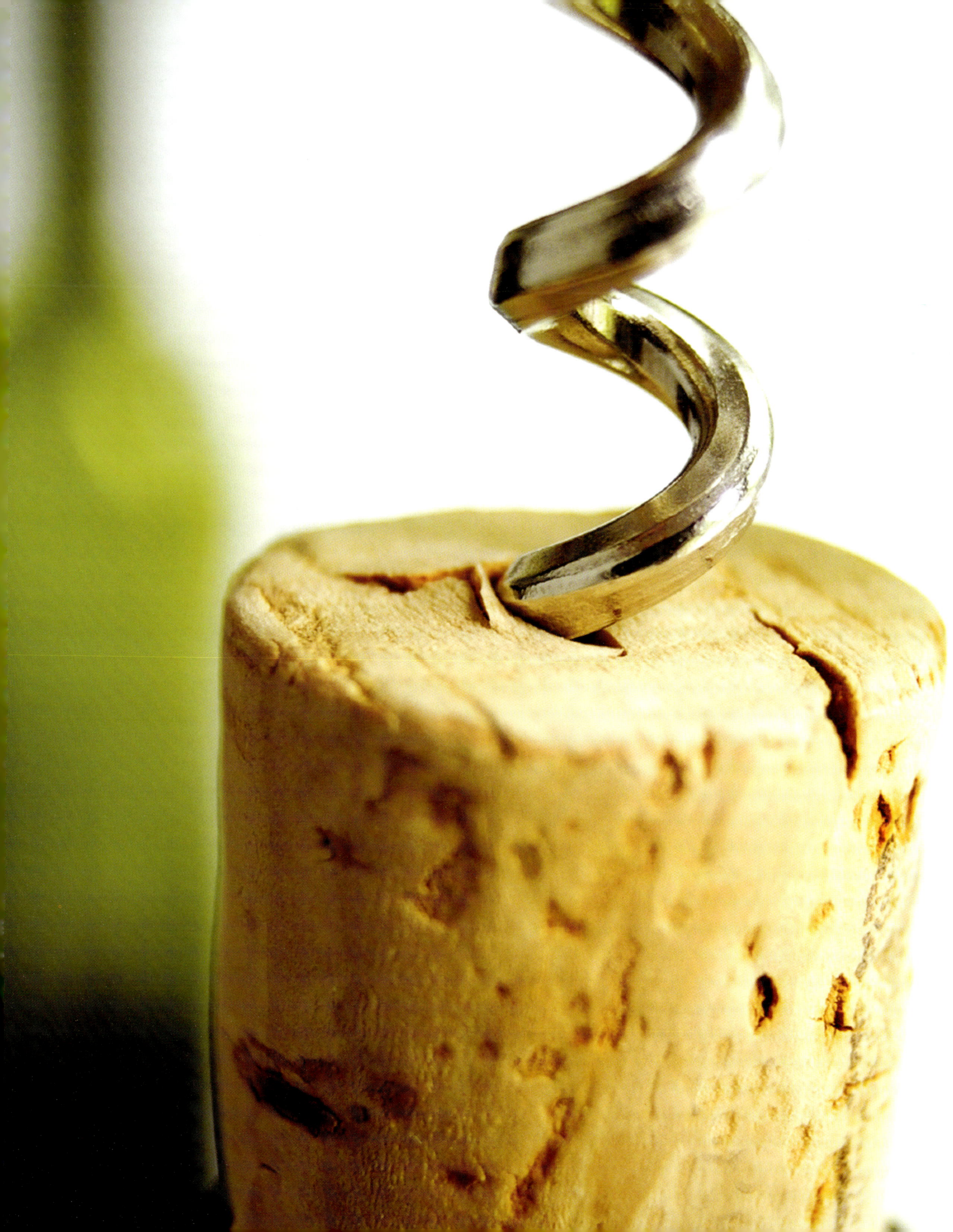

# Between Madeira and La Mancha

It is sometimes said that the term 'New World' implies a certain state of mind of the winemaker's rather than a geographic definition. This might be enough justification for placing Malta in the New World spotlight, although on the map, Malta is of course situated in the Old World of wine.

Although the vine has always had a natural place in Malta and Maltese people have made wine for centuries, as is the case in most New World countries, the modern Maltese wine industry has only recently enjoyed a great revival in the cellar and vineyard. The area under vine in Malta and Gozo is about one tenth of New Zealand's national vineyard and very tiny compared to any region in Europe. But, as in other New World countries, Malta's winemakers have enjoyed the same refreshing freedom and manoeuvrability and they have been very innovative and creative in their approach to viticulture and winemaking.

Experiments abound, with French and American oak barriques, for example, and with anything that helps to capture those elusive fruit flavours of the grape. Malta now has a small number of successful wineries able to compete not only on supermarket shelves, but also on airlines bringing many tourists to the sunny Maltese Islands, as well as in budding export markets.
Whilst developing an appellation system, originally taking Italy and France as role models, just like New World producers, Maltese winemakers have had to adapt methods to their own climates. More importantly, as in new emerging winemaking countries, Maltese vintners, too, have questioned what the consumer wants and have successfully produced highly marketable wines. Maltese winemakers have now embarked on a course of renewal that is unparalleled in their craft's history, ancient or modern. They are underpinning the reputation of their wines and pressing on to create innovative wines that are gaining international acclaim.

The temptation to produce more and more familiar, safe wine without much character is always there, but a handful of quality vintners in Malta seem to withstand the insidious trend towards wine-by-formula. They are drawing from a diverse palette of grapes to create unique wines that please different palates. This has come about at a time when basic winemaking technology and skills and hence wine quality has improved immeasurably. The result is wine that is interesting without being intimidating. Yet, ultimately novelty is not enough and it will be perceived quality and real value as much as genuine varietal content that will shape the future of Malta grown wine.

In this respect, it will be interesting to see whether the Maltese vintners will also bank some of their oenological future on the further development and use of the native varieties, Girgentina and Ġellewża.

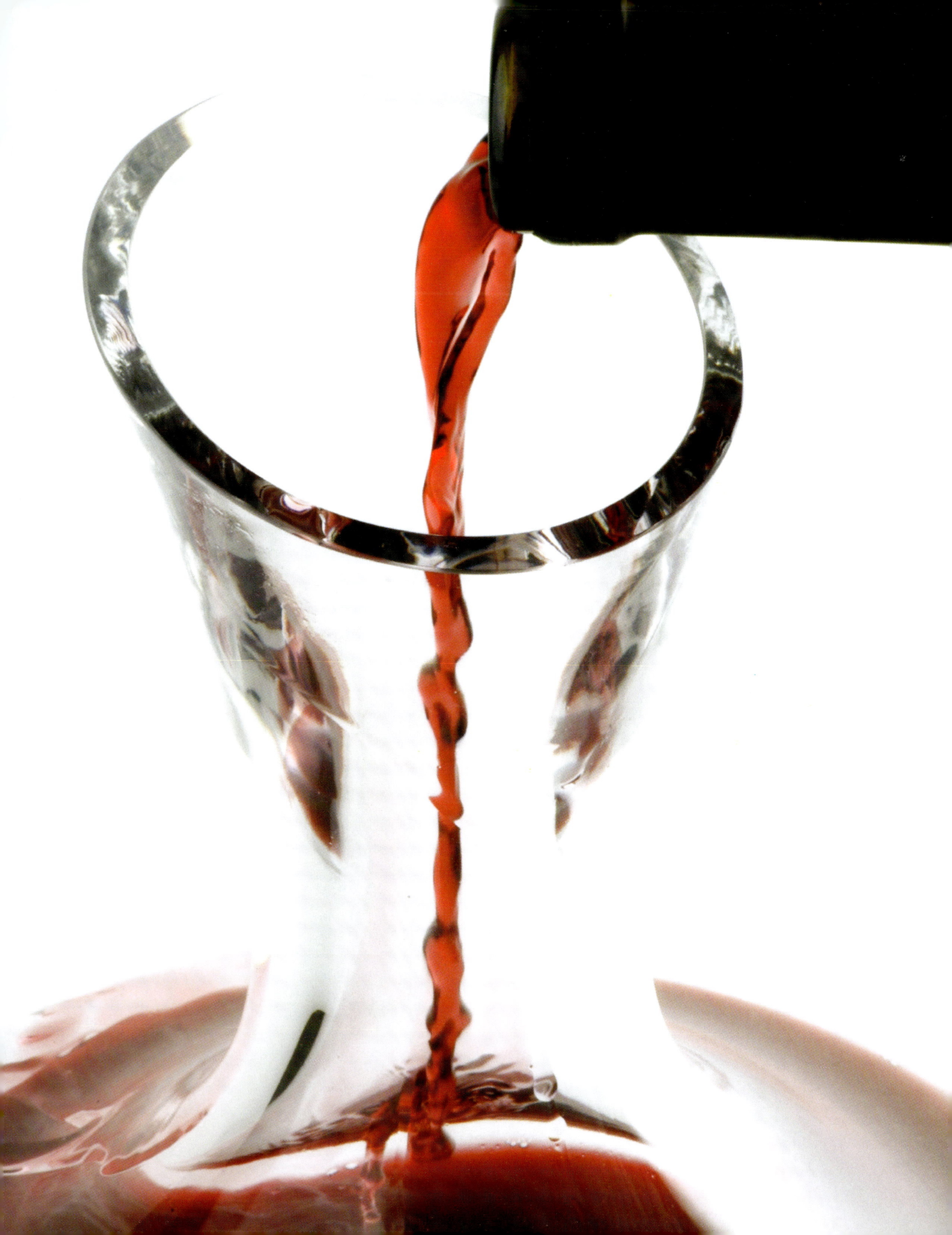

If nothing else, the wines made from them are unique and should appeal to wine lovers who are seeking new horizons.

Just on the other side of the Mediterranean Sea, Sicilian and Sardinian winemakers can boast a proud tradition in sporting their indigenous grapes. The smaller scenic Italian islands of Ischia and Capri, too, keep on producing famous wines from native varieties that are believed to be direct descendants of vines cultivated by the Romans and probably also by the Greeks before them.

In Malta, the tiring debate as to what is acceptable – indigenous or international – seems to have come to a close.
If anything, it has actually gone on for far too long. There should be no squabble: just a commitment from the vigneron to grow the best possible grapes, native or not, for the winemaker to make the best quality wine possible.

It is good to see that the choice of Malta grown wines has never been greater and keeps on growing whilst winemaking standards have never been higher.
For those to whom Maltese wines are new, reading this book should make the choice easier.

Hopefully, before laying this book aside and rushing off to uncork a bottle, you, the reader, will prepare for your reference shelves a fresh wine region file, which will fit snugly in between Madeira and La Mancha…

Sahha!

BETWEEN MADEIRA AND LA MANCHA

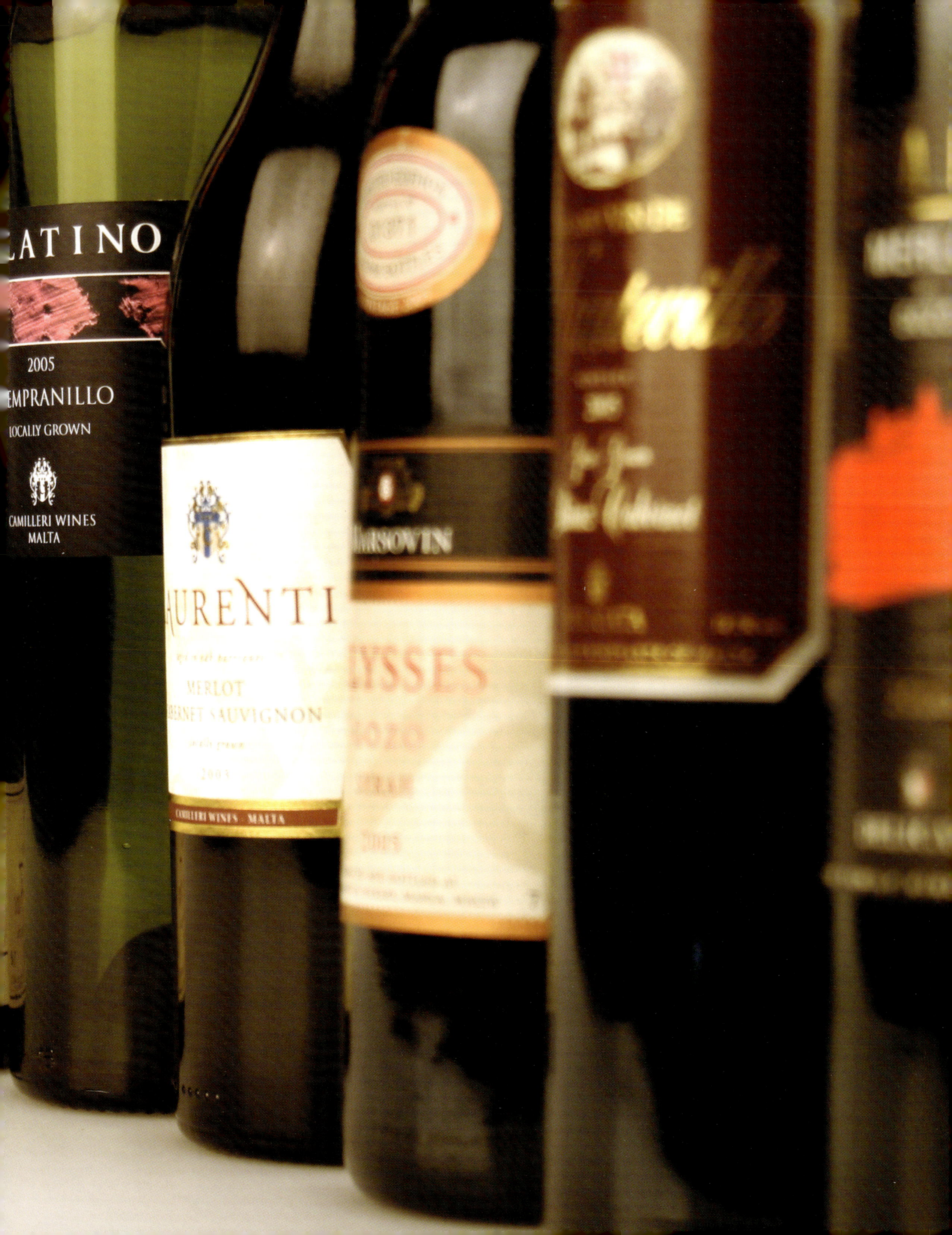
2005
CAMILLERI WINES
MALTA
MERLOT
CAMILLERI WINES · MALTA

● Marsovin  ● Meridiana  ● Camilleri  ● Delicata

S - Single Varietal   B - Blend

## White, rosé and sparkling wines

| Name | Tasting Cue | Origin | Oak | Girgentina | Chardonnay | Sauvignon Blanc | Pinot Bianco | Grenache | Carignan | Gellewza | Merlot | Syrah | Temp °C |
|---|---|---|---|---|---|---|---|---|---|---|---|---|---|
| Cassar de Malte | Richly dry full-sparkling white | Malta | | | S | | | | | | | | 6-9 |
| 1919 White | Flavoursome, buttery dry white | Malta | O | B | B | | | | | | | | 11-13 |
| Antonin Blanc | Gently toasted, lime & appley dry white | Gozo | O | | B | | B | | | | | | 13-15 |
| Odyssey | Enchanting, spicy dry rosé | Malta | | | S | | | S | | | | | 8-11 |
| Mistral | Mature and full-bodied dry white | Malta | O | | S | | | | | | | | 13-15 |
| Isis | Delicately perfumed and rich chard-true white | Malta | | | S | | | | | | | | 12-14 |
| Palatino Chardonnay | Citrussy, medium-bodied white | Malta | | | S | | | | | | | | 8-11 |
| Laurenti White | Mature, fat oaky dry white | Malta | O | | S | | | | | | | | 13-15 |
| Zigland White | Sweet pea-scented, light bodied dry white wine | Malta | | B | B | | | | | | | | 8-11 |
| Zigland Rosé | Likeable enough dry rosé | Malta | | | | | | B | B | | | | 8-11 |
| Blush | Edgy, floral-like dry rosé | Malta | | | | | | | | | B | B | 8-11 |
| Girgentina Frizzante (NV) | Semi-sparkling, bone dry white. | Malta | | S | | | | | | | | | 8-11 |
| Gellewza Frizzante (NV) | Semi-sparkling, strawberryish medium-dry rosé | Malta | | | | | | | | S | | | 8-11 |
| Fior del Mondo White | Flinty and mouthwatering, light-bodied wine | Malta | | S | | | | S | | | | | 8-11 |
| Medina Vineyards Rosé | Elegant, aromatic, rose-petally dry rosé | Malta | | | | | | | | | | | 8-11 |
| Medina Vineyards White | Crisp and floral dry white wine | Malta | | B | B | | | | | | | | 8-11 |
| Medina Vineyards Chardonnay | Clean and lean, tropical-flavoured dry white | Malta | | | S | | | | | | | | 11-13 |
| Victoria Heights Chardonnay | Delicately oaky and honeyed dry white | Gozo | O | | S | | | | | | | | 12-14 |
| Gran Cavalier Sauvignon Blanc | Kiwi- and gooseberry-laced dry white wine | Malta | | | | S | | | | | | | 10-12 |
| Gran Cavalier Chardonnay | Elegant, round & lenghty full-bodied dry white | Malta | O | | S | | | | | | | | 13-15 |
| Grand Vin de Hauteville Chardonnay | Fruit-crammed, oaky dry white | Malta | O | | S | | | | | | | | 13-15 |

# Reds for drinking - or keeping

| Name | Tasting Cue | Origin | Oak | Petit Verdot | Merlot | Cabernet Sauvignon | Syrah / Shiraz | Cabernet Franc | Grenache | Carignan | Gellewza | Tempranillo | Temp °C |
|---|---|---|---|---|---|---|---|---|---|---|---|---|---|
| Ulysses Red | Medium-bodied, firm grained spicy red | Gozo | O | | | | S | | | | | | 14-16 |
| 1919 Red | Old-fashioned peppery, clove & raspberry-ish red | Malta | O | | B | B | B | | | | B | | 14-16 |
| Antonin Noir | Velvety, full-bodied red in the bordeaux style | Malta | O | | B | B | | B | | | | | 16-18 |
| Marnisi | Delightful old-world tobacco 'n blueberry red | Malta | O | B | B | B | | B | | | | | 16-18 |
| Cheval Franc | Lovely leafy, cedary italianate characterful red | Malta | O | | | | | | | | | | 15-17 |
| Grand Maitre | Traditional, classy full-bodied dry red wine | Malta | O | | B | B | B | B | | | | | 16-18 |
| Melqart | Well-balanced, forest-fruitish full-bodied red | Malta | O | | B | B | | | | | | | 16-18 |
| Nexus | Deliciously rich-plummy, silky hang-on-to red | Malta | | | S | | S | | | | | | 17-19 |
| Bel | Classic, barnyardy medium-bodied red | Malta | O | | | S | | | | | | | 17-19 |
| Celsius | Linear, dried currant, characterful big red | Malta | O | | | S | | | | | | | 17-19 |
| Palatino Cabernet | Juicy and fruit cab | Malta | | | | | | | | | | | 14-16 |
| Palatino Syrah | Straight, vibrant purple red | Malta | | | | | S | | | | | | 14-16 |
| Palatino Tempranillo | Lifted, fruity yet shy young red | Malta | | | | | | | | | | S | 14-16 |
| Palatino Merlot | Medum-bodied, blood plummy red | Malta | | | S | | | | | | | | 14-16 |
| Zigland Red | Cheerful, easy-drinking red | Malta | | | B | B | B | | | | | | 14-16 |
| Laurenti Red | Lovely cigar-box, dark, dense, fleshy palate-filler | Malta | O | | | B | | | | | | | 17-19 |
| Fior Del Mondo Gellewza | Cherryish, stone-crunchy featherweight red | Malta | | | | | | | B | | S | | 12-14 |
| Medina Vineyards Red | Herb-infused, juicy light-bodied red | Malta | | | | | B | | | B | | | 12-14 |
| Medina Vineyards Syrah Superior | Upfront, leatherly medium-bodied red | Malta | | | | | S | | | | | | 14-16 |
| Medina Vineyards Cabernet Sauvignon | Easier-going with uplifting red fruit flavours | Malta | | | | S | | | | | | | 14-16 |
| Medina Vineyards Merlot | Smooth, toffeeish, medium-bodied red | Malta | | | S | | | | | | | | 15-17 |
| Victoria Heights Merlot | Smokey-spicily medium-bodied example | Gozo | O | | S | | | | | | | | 16-18 |
| Gran Cavalier Syrah | Gamey rhone-look-alike, complex red | Malta | O | | | | S | | | | | | 16-18 |
| Gran Cavalier Cabernet Merlot | Fine tabacco-cassis-cedar claret like red | Malta | O | | B | B | | | | | | | 17-19 |
| Grand Vin de Hauteville Cabernet Sauvignon | Classy and intense blackcurranty big red | Malta | O | | S | S | | | | | | | 17-19 |
| Grand Vin de Hauteville Shiraz Cabernet | Weighty, bold yet silky full-bodied red | Malta | O | | | B | B | | | | | | 17-19 |

# How To Find Out More

**MALTESE WINERIES**

CAMILLERI WINES
Oratory Street,
Naxxar NXR 03,
MALTA
Tel: (356) 21 412 391
Website: www.camilleriwines.com
e-mail: info@camilleriwines.com

EMMANUEL DELICATA WINEMAKER
The Winery on the Waterfront,
Paola PLA 08,
MALTA
Tel: (356) 21 825 199
Website: www.delicata.com
e-mail: info@delicata.com

MARSOVIN
The Winery - Wills Street,
Paola PLA 01,
MALTA
Tel: (356) 21 824 920
Website: www.marsovin.com
e-mail: info@marsovin.com.mt

MERIDIANA WINE ESTATE
Ta' Qali BZN 09,
MALTA
Tel: (356) 21 413 550
Website: www.meridiana.com.mt
e-mail: info@meridiana.com.mt

MONTEKRISTO
Château d'If,
Hal Farruġ Road,
Luqa LQA 05,
MALTA
Tel: (356) 21 231 448
Website: www.montekristo.com
e-mail: info@montekristo.com

**WINE COURSES IN MALTA**

MCAST
Corradino Hill, Paola PLA 08, MALTA.
www.mcast.edu.mt
Evening classes on viticulture and oenology for keen amateurs led by Maltese teachers.

MEDITERRANEAN WINE CAMPUS
Looza, Kwartier ta' Xindi, San Gwann SGN 08, MALTA, www.winecampus.org
Certified and carefully structured wine (trade) courses, including wine tasting sessions, at all levels and about all regions including Malta. Also delivered via distance learning.

WINE AND SPIRIT EDUCATION TRUST
39-45 Bermondsey Street, London, SE1 3XF, UK, www.wset.co.uk
Standard wine courses organised worldwide and also delivered at the Institute for Tourism Studies as approved programme provider in Malta.

**MINISTRY FOR RURAL AFFAIRS AND THE ENVIRONMENT - MALTA**

OFFICIAL AGRICULTURAL RESEARCH AND DEVELOPMENT CENTRE
Ghammieri, MALTA
Tel: (356) 25 904 151
Website: www.agric.gov.mt/viticulture.htm
e-mail: randall.caruana@gov.mt

# Bibliography And Further Reading

**WINE IN GENERAL**

Amerine, M.A. & Roessler, E.B. *Wines, Their Sensory Evaluation* (2nd edition), W.H. Freeman, 1983.

Anderson, B. *The Mitchell Beazley Pocket Guide to Italian Wines*, Mitchell Beazley, 1984.

Basset, G. *The Wine Experience*, Kyle Cathie Limited, 2000.

Beckkett, F. *Wine by Style*, Mitchell Beazley, 1998.

Belfrage, N. *Life beyond Lambrusco*, Sigwick & Jackson, 1985.

Brook, S. *Sauvignon Blanc & Semillon*, Viking, 1992.

Clarke, O. *New Classic Wines*, Websters/Mitchell Beazley, 1991.

Dubs, S. *Les Vins d'Alsace*, Robert Laffont, 1991.

Enjalbert, H. *Les Grands Vins de Saint Emilion*, Pomerol et Fronsac, Editions Bardi, 1983.

Galet, P. A *Practical Ampelography – Grapevine Identification*, Cornell University Press, 1979.

Gluck, M. *The Sensational Liquid*, Hodder & Stoughton, 1999.

Halliday, J. & Jarratt R. *The Wines & History of The Hunter Valley*, McGraw-Hill, 1979.

MacDonogh, G. *Syrah, Grenache and Mouvedre*, Viking, 1992.

Peynaud, E. *Connaissance et Travail du Vin* (2nd edition), Dunod, 1984.

Philips, R. *A Short History of Wine*, HarperCollins, 2002.

Robinson, J. *Vines, Grapes & Wines*, Mitchell Beazley, 2005.

Robinson, J. *Jancis Robinson's Wine Course*, BBC Books, 1995.

Robinson, J. *The Oxford Companion to Wine* (2nd edition), Oxford University Press, 1999.

Waldin, M. *Organic Wine Guide*, Thorsons, 1999.

Winkler, A.J. *General Viticulture*, University of California Press, 1974.

Schuster, M. *Essential Winetasting*, Mitchell Beazley, 2005.

Wilson, J.E. *Terroir*, Mitchell Beazley, 2004.

Zoecklein, B. *Méthode Champenoise, Viticultural Considerations*, Practical Winery, May/June 1985.

## MALTESE WINE AND FOOD REFERENCES

Anonymous, *Wine Making Sector Study,* IPSE, 2001.

Anonymous, *Wine Act* (CAP. 436) *Classification of Vine Varieties (Production of Wine Grapes)* No. 17,965, 5th September 2006, Regulations, Government Gazette of Malta, 2006.

Borg, G. *On Viticulture and Vintners,* Options Méditerrannéennes, CIHEAM-IAMM, 1993.

Borg. J. *Wirt L-Għassara ta' L-Għeneb,* Ministry of Agriculture, Malta, 1996.

Cremona, M. *Maltese Olive Oil,* Proximus Publishing, 2002.

Cremona, M. *A Year in the Country: Life and Food in Rural Malta,* Proximus Publishing, 2003.

Dunbar Cousin, G.J. & Peralta, G.J. *The Reconstruction of Rootstock in Local Viticulture,* Dept. of Agriculture, Malta, 1961.

Hodder, A.J. *Pre-Assessment of Potential for Improvement and Intensification of Wine Grape Viticulture in Malta,* FAO, 1997.

Mattei, P. *25 Years in a Maltese Kitchen,* Miranda Publications, 2003.

Miceli-Farruġia, M. *Coping with Scarcity,* The Management Journal, MIM, June 2001.

Olmo, H.P. *Grape and Wine Production in the Maltese Islands,* FAO, 1963.

Schembri, P.J. *Physical Geography and Ecology of the Maltese Islands,* Options Méditerrannéennes, CIHEAM-IAMM, 1993.

## (ONLINE) MAGAZINES & (MALTESE) MEDIA

Decanter, www.decanter.com

Harpers, www.harpers-wine.com

Wine (and Spirit Magazine) International, www.wineint.com

Wine Business Monthly, www.winebusiness.com

The Malta Independent, www.independent.com.mt

MaltaToday, www.maltatoday.com.mt

The Times and Sunday Times of Malta, www.timesofmalta.com

Malta's Food Critic 'Mona', www.planetmona.com

## CREDITS

The publisher and author would like to thank the following organisations and persons for their kind assistance and permission to reproduce their photographs: Camilleri Wines, Emmanuel Delicata Winemaker, Marsovin Ltd, Meridiana Wine Estate, Vivai Cooperativi Rauscedo, Dr. Edric Bonello and Bill Hermitage.

Every effort has been made to trace the copyright holders. We apologise in advance for any unintentional omissions and we would be pleased to insert the appropriate acknowledgement in any subsequent edition.

The publisher and author also thank Marc Spiteri for coordinating Serge Dubs' foreword in French and Living Interiors (www.livinginteriors.com.mt) for the loan of the Riedel stemware and wine paraphernalia.

# Index

Acidity  59, 62, 83, 87, 92, 99, 108
Alcoholic strength  73, 75
Ansonica  76
Attack  93

Barriques  77, 89, 101, 120
Blends  29, 57 ,77, 97, 101, 102, 111
Body  52, 99
Bush trained  18, 78, 88

Cabernet Franc  96, 99, 102
Cabernet Sauvignon  44, 50, 52, 79, 83, 96, 101
Camilleri Wines  38, 44, 55, 59, 84, 91, 97
Carignan  50, 79, 83, 85,  111
Catarratto  76
Census of Agriculture  42
Chardonnay  16, 18, 20, 44, 50 ,55, 59, 77,88, 89, 95, 113
Chardonnay du Monde  45
Clones  24, 50, 57, 73
Coleiro Wine Company  34
Colour  20, 27, 38, 45, 58, 75, 83, 90, 96, 103, 116
Comino  12, 18, 87
Consumption (per capita)  34, 67

Denominazione di Origine Controllata (DOC)  16, 62
Denominazzjoni ta' Oriġni Kontrollata (DOK)  62
Domestic demand  47
Dureza  81

Emmanuel Delicata  38, 44, 45, 55, 93, 126

Farmer's wine  35, 37
Farmers Wine Co-operative Society  35
Field blends  29
Frascati  45
Frizzante  76, 78, 109

Garganega  77
Ġellewża  18, 22, 29, 30, 43, 50, 58, 72, 75, 78, 83, 109
Girgentina  18, 22, 29, 30, 42, 50, 58, 72, 75, 88, 90, 95, 108
Gouais Blanc  89
Gozo  12, 18, 24, 30, 37, 42, 55, 72, 89, 91, 96, 102, 106, 114
Grenache  50, 79, 83,87, 110, 111, 127

Habitat  16
Harvesting  22

Indicazione Geografica Tipica (IGT)  66
Indigenous (grape) varieties  20, 50, 53, 68, 72, 77
International (grape) varieties  18, 20, 43, 48, 50, 52, 55
International awards  45
International Organisation of the Vine and Wine (OIV)  68
Inzolia  76
Irrigation  14, 18, 20, 57, 72

Land fragmentation  18

Malta grown (wines)  48, 50, 55, 68, 75, 80, 90,96, 101, 106, 110, 122
Malta Wines & Vines Association  52
Mammolo  75
Marsovin  38, 44, 47, 52, 55, 58, 84, 88, 91, 97, 102
Mediterranean (Sea)  12, 19, 29, 38, 52, 80, 89, 93, 99, 103, 122
Meridiana (Wine Estate) 38, 55, 59, 84, 91, 97, 102
Méritage  59, 99
Merlot  18, 20, 44, 50, 58, 79, 83, 96, 101, 114
Mondeuse Blanc  81
Moscato  44, 50, 79, 80, 103

Mouthfeel  75, 96
Muscat (family)  80, 102

Native (grape) varieties  18, 30, 32, 43, 50, 70, 78, 120
New World  77, 90, 93, 96, 99, 120
New-wave Maltese wines  37, 79
Nose  58, 75, 83, 87, 102, 106, 110

Oak (-aged)  75, 77, 83, 89, 91, 101, 113, 120
Unoak(ed)  45, 81, 84, 101
Oenology  13, 57, 126
Old World  29, 120

Palate  45, 47, 74, 87, 90, 101, 108, 114
Petit Verdot  50, 99
Phylloxera  30, 50, 72
Pinot Bianco  44, 59, 92
Pinot Grigio  45, 77
Pinot Noir  16, 89
Planting  20, 24, 33, 48, 52, 55, 58, 79, 81, 88
Private Estate Selection Wines  59

Quality control  68

Rhône Rangers  83
Rhône varieties  79
Riedel  106
Rootstock  24, 33, 50, 53 128
Rosé (wines)  55, 76, 78, 85, 102, 109
Ruby Cabernet  52, 102
Rural planning  27

Sauvignon Blanc  20, 44, 45, 50, 77, 88, 93, 99, 127
Serving temperatures  106, 121
Shiraz  81, 84, 101, 102, 115
Single varietal wine  45, 47, 87, 90
Soave  45, 77

Soil type(s)  24, 81, 89
Super Maltese  79
Syrah  16, 50, 58, 79, 81, 96, 99, 101, 111, 115, 127

Tannin (s)  20, 75, 81, 99, 110, 115
Tempranillo  50, 101
Terroir  42, 55, 79, 81, 127
Texture  20, 24, 83, 96, 108, 113
Trebbiano  44
Typicity  42, 58, 79, 96, 106, 108

Varietal character  76, 81, 101
Vine and Research Station  33
Vine training  18
Vines for Wines  55, 56, 58
Vinification  37, 52, 55, 62, 75, 85, 101
Vintage  19, 35, 44, 57, 76, 93, 96, 111, 115
Viognier  50, 77, 79, 87, 88
Viticulture  12, 16, 27, 37, 62, 120, 126
Vitis vinifera  31, 50

Wine Act  62, 68, 128
Winegrowing  37, 62

Yields  19, 20, 53, 59, 77, 83, 97